TRUE FACTS THAT SOUND LIKE Bull$#*t SPORTS

500 GAME-CHANGING FACTS FROM OUT OF LEFT FIELD

SHANE CARLEY

CIDER MILL PRESS
BOOK PUBLISHERS

Cider Mill Press Book Publishers
"Where good books are ready for press"
501 Nelson Place
Nashville, Tennessee 37214

cidermillpress.com

Typography: Adobe Caslon Pro, Festivo Letters No1, Capriccio, Microbrew One, Trade Gothic LT Std

Illustrations by Rebecca Pry

Printed in the United States of America
24 25 26 27 28 VER 5 4 3 2 1

First Edition

[CONTENTS]

[Introduction]

In the world of sports, something unbelievable happens just about every week. Sometimes it's an individual performance that makes you sit up and say, "Wow!" Other times, it's a blunder that leaves you hanging your head. And still other times, it's a reminder that athletes are just like the rest of us: goofy, flawed, and, ultimately, human. Sports are a microcosm of the human condition. They evoke joy, sadness, disappointment, incredulity, elation, anger, and every other emotion in the span of just a few hours. Whether you're a baseball fan, a soccer enthusiast, or a water polo junkie, there's always excitement to be found in sports.

This book is filled with 500 facts about football, baseball, basketball, hockey, and more. Did you know a quarterback has thrown a touchdown pass to himself not once, but twice? Have you heard about the New York Yankees pitchers who swapped families? Or the soccer star who left his Porsche at a train station and promptly forgot about it? And did you know about the Formula One racer who filled a rival's hotel room with frogs before a race? You may think you know your favorite sport, but this book is sure to contain a fact or two that will shock and amaze you. So let's forego the coin toss, skip the kickoff, and dive right in!

[American Football]

Did you know that the Canadian Football League (CFL) is actually older than the National Football League (NFL)? Maybe it should be called "Canadian football" instead of "American football." Whatever the case, football is a long and storied sport that has had its fair share of characters over the years. Legendary talents like Tom Brady and Jerry Rice have amazed viewers for decades, while players like Lawrence Taylor and Ronnie Lott have given new meaning to the term "tough." Featuring incredible comebacks and historic blunders, this section lays bare the highs and lows of America's most popular game.

1. IN 1983, OLIVER LUCK TOOK OVER THE HOUSTON STARTING QUARTERBACK JOB FROM ARCHIE MANNING. DECADES LATER, HIS SON ANDREW WOULD TAKE THE COLTS' STARTING QUARTERBACK JOB FROM ARCHIE'S SON, PEYTON.

2. MOST PEOPLE WOULD CONSIDER BOBBY LAYNE AND MATTHEW STAFFORD THE BEST QUARTERBACKS THE DETROIT LIONS HAVE EVER HAD, WHICH MAKES IT EVEN STRANGER THAT THEY WENT TO THE SAME HIGH SCHOOL AND EVEN LIVED ON THE SAME DALLAS STREET.

3. IN SUPER BOWL LI, THE NEW ENGLAND PATRIOTS OVERCAME A 28–3 DEFICIT TO DEFEAT THE ATLANTA FALCONS IN OVERTIME.

   The 25-point comeback was the largest in Super Bowl history—in fact, no other team has come back from more than ten points down in a Super Bowl.

4. THE BUFFALO BILLS ARE THE ONLY NFL TEAM TO APPEAR IN FOUR CONSECUTIVE SUPER BOWLS...AND THEY LOST ALL FOUR.

5. SUPER BOWL XLVII WAS PLAYED BETWEEN THE BALTIMORE RAVENS AND THE SAN FRANCISCO 49ERS, WHO WERE COACHED BY TWO BROTHERS: JOHN AND JIM HARBAUGH.

   (John's Ravens won, 34–31.)

6. IN THE MIDDLE OF SUPER BOWL XLVII, THE STADIUM SUFFERED A POWER OUTAGE, LEADING TO A STOPPAGE OF PLAY THAT LASTED MORE THAN 30 MINUTES.

7. IN 1983, STEELERS QUARTERBACK TERRY BRADSHAW CHECKED HIMSELF INTO A HOSPITAL UNDER AN ASSUMED NAME.
The name? Tom Brady.

8. IN 1943, SO MANY EAGLES AND STEELERS PLAYERS WERE SERVING IN WWII THAT THE TWO TEAMS WERE FORCED TO TEMPORARILY MERGE, FORMING THE "PHILADELPHIA-PITTSBURGH STEAGLES."
The team went 5-4-1 and just missed the playoffs.

9. THE YEAR AFTER MERGING WITH THE EAGLES, THE STEELERS JOINED FORCES WITH THE CHICAGO CARDINALS TO FORM A TEAM CALLED "CARD-PITT."
Unfortunately, the team failed to win a single game, going 0–10 and earning the nickname "Car-Pitt," or "carpet," from sportswriters.

10. IN 1916, THE GEORGIA TECH FOOTBALL TEAM DEFEATED CUMBERLAND COLLEGE 222-0.
It is (by far) the largest margin of victory in the history of college and professional football.

• 11 •

HALL OF FAME QUARTERBACK BRETT FAVRE'S FIRST NFL COMPLETION WAS CAUGHT BY... BRETT FAVRE!

The ball was batted at the line of scrimmage and wound up back in Favre's hands. In 2023, Texans rookie C. J. Stroud replicated the unlikely feat, catching his own first pass against the Baltimore Ravens.

· 12 ·

IN 1896, A MEN'S SOCIAL CLUB ORGANIZED AN EXHIBITION MATCH BETWEEN TWO FOOTBALL TEAMS CONSISTING OF FIVE WOMEN EACH.

While the game started just fine, the local police stepped in and put a stop to the match, citing the danger created by unruly spectators.

13. LEGENDARY CARDINALS WIDE RECEIVER LARRY FITZGERALD—WHO, IT CANNOT BE EMPHASIZED ENOUGH, DID NOT PLAY DEFENSE—FINISHED HIS CAREER WITH MORE TACKLES (41) THAN DROPPED PASSES (29).

14. IN 2014, THE KANSAS CITY CHIEFS BECAME THE FIRST TEAM SINCE 1964 TO COMPLETE AN ENTIRE SEASON WITHOUT THROWING A TOUCHDOWN PASS TO A WIDE RECEIVER.

15. IT TOOK VIKINGS WIDE RECEIVER JUSTIN JEFFERSON JUST 52 GAMES TO RECORD MORE RECEIVING YARDS THAN ANY CHICAGO BEARS RECEIVER IN THE TEAM'S 100+ YEAR HISTORY.

16. IN 2023, THE AFC AND NFC PRO BOWL TEAMS WERE EACH COACHED BY A FEMALE OFFENSIVE COORDINATOR.
Diana Flores and Vanita Krouch are two flag football legends and were brought in by the league in a bid for greater representation and inclusivity.

17. THE BUCCANEERS WERE FOUNDED IN 1974, BUT IT TOOK 32 SEASONS AND 1,865 ATTEMPTS BEFORE THE TEAM EVER RETURNED A KICKOFF FOR A TOUCHDOWN.
Michael Spurlock finally did the honors in 2007.

18. AMY TRASK WAS THE FIRST WOMAN TO SERVE AS CEO OF AN NFL TEAM, FILLING THE ROLE FOR THE OAKLAND RAIDERS FROM 1997 TO 2013. SHE WAS GIVEN THE NICKNAME "THE PRINCESS OF DARKNESS" BY FANS AND COLLEAGUES, WHICH SHE EVENTUALLY CAME TO EMBRACE.

Trask remains influential in the world of sports, and recently served as CEO of a 3-on-3 basketball league cofounded by rapper Ice Cube.

19. THE RAIDERS HAVE CONTINUED TO LEAD THE WAY WHEN IT COMES TO REPRESENTATION: IN 2022, AMY TRASK BECAME THE FIRST BLACK WOMAN TO SERVE AS PRESIDENT OF A TEAM.

She is only the third woman to ever hold such a role.

20. IN 1982, A KICKER WAS NAMED THE NFL'S MOST VALUABLE PLAYER.

It was a strike-shortened season, but still.

21. A QUARTERBACK HAS THROWN A TOUCHDOWN PASS TO HIMSELF TWICE IN NFL HISTORY.

Vikings quarterback Brad Johnson first accomplished the feat in 1997, and Titans quarterback Marcus Mariota did it again in 2018.

22. THE 2008 DETROIT LIONS WON ALL FOUR OF THEIR PRESEASON GAMES...THEN WENT ON TO LOSE ALL 16 OF THEIR REGULAR SEASON GAMES.

• 23 •

NEW YORK JETS QUARTERBACK MARK SANCHEZ ONCE FUMBLED THE FOOTBALL AFTER RUNNING DIRECTLY INTO THE REAR END OF HIS OFFENSIVE LINEMAN.

The play famously became known as "The Butt Fumble."

· 24 ·

THERE WERE NO FEMALE COACHES IN THE NFL UNTIL 2015, WHEN DR. JEN WELTER BECAME A COACHING INTERN FOR THE ARIZONA CARDINALS.

As of the writing of this book, there are now 12 women in full-time coaching roles throughout the league.

25. PATRIOTS SPECIAL TEAMER LARRY IZZO ONCE (ALLEGEDLY) RECEIVED A GAME BALL FROM COACH BILL BELICHICK AS A TONGUE-IN-CHEEK REWARD FOR, AH, "GOING NUMBER TWO" ON THE SIDELINES DURING A GAME WITHOUT ANYONE NOTICING.

26. THERE WAS A WOMEN'S PROFESSIONAL FOOTBALL LEAGUE AS FAR BACK AS 1965.

The Women's Professional American Football League operated from 1965 to 1973 and included teams in Cleveland, Pittsburgh, Toronto, and Detroit. The league was briefly revived from 1999 to 2007.

27. IN 1950, CHICAGO CARDINALS QUARTERBACK JIM HARDY SET AN NFL RECORD BY THROWING EIGHT INTERCEPTIONS IN ONE GAME.

The very next week, he tied the NFL record for most touchdowns thrown in a game (at the time, six).

28. ONLY THREE PLAYERS IN NFL HISTORY HAVE CAUGHT A PASS WHILE OVER THE AGE OF 40.

Jerry Rice caught 161 passes for 2,169 yards after turning 40, while Tom Brady had one catch for 6 yards. Brett Favre also had one catch...for -2 yards.

29. IN 1976, A SMALL PLANE CRASHED INTO BALTIMORE MEMORIAL STADIUM JUST MINUTES AFTER A PLAYOFF GAME BETWEEN THE RAVENS AND STEELERS HAD ENDED.

Fortunately, no one was seriously hurt (not even the pilot).

30. DURING A GAME IN 2002, THE STEELERS OUTGAINED THE TEXANS 422 YARDS TO 47. SOMEHOW, THEY LOST THE GAME 24-6.

31. IN 1932, THE CHICAGO BEARS TIED AN INCREDIBLE THREE CONSECUTIVE GAMES. WHILE TIES WERE MORE COMMON BACK THEN, THREE IN A ROW WAS STILL UNHEARD OF—AND GIVEN THE RARITY OF TIES TODAY, IT'S A FEAT THAT WILL ALMOST CERTAINLY NEVER BE DUPLICATED.

Perhaps worst of all? Each game ended 0–0.

32. HALL OF FAME QUARTERBACK SAMMY BAUGH ONCE THREW FOUR TOUCHDOWNS IN A GAME ON OFFENSE AND INTERCEPTED FOUR OF THE OPPOSING QUARTERBACK'S PASSES ON DEFENSE.

33. IN 2016, THE DIVISIONAL-ROUND MATCHUP BETWEEN THE PACKERS AND CARDINALS WENT TO OVERTIME. REFEREE CLETE BLAKEMAN CONDUCTED THE COIN FLIP...ONLY THE COIN DIDN'T FLIP.

It remained flat for the duration of its flight, prompting outrage from the Packers and, ultimately, a redo of the toss (what could have been a controversy ended up being a moot point: the Cardinals won both tosses).

34. ONE OF THE LONGEST PUNTS IN NFL HISTORY WAS BOOTED NOT BY A PUNTER, BUT BY A QUARTERBACK.

Eagles quarterback Randall Cunningham kicked a 91-yard punt during a game against the Giants in 1989.

• 35 •

PITTSBURGH PIRATES
RUNNING BACK BYRON
"WHIZZER" WHITE WON
THE NFL RUSHING TITLE
IN 1938. IN 1962, HE
EARNED A DIFFERENT
TITLE: UNITED STATES
SUPREME COURT JUSTICE.

BEYOND THIS POINT

• 36 •

THERE IS A RULE PROHIBITING THE USE OF A PLOW TO CLEAR SNOW FROM THE FIELD DURING A GAME.

Why? Because in 1982, the Patriots used a plow to clear space on a snowbound field to kick the winning field goal in a game that would ultimately end 3–0.

37. AS OF PUBLICATION, THERE ARE NO WOMEN ENSHRINED IN THE PRO FOOTBALL HALL OF FAME.

However, four women have been inducted into the American Football Association Hall of Fame, which recognizes the accomplishments of minor league and semipro players.

38. THE LONGEST NON-SCORING PLAY IN NFL HISTORY WAS 104 YARDS.

Vikings kick returner Percy Harvin received a kickoff 7 yards deep in the end zone and ran over 100 yards before being tackled at the 3-yard line by Falcons cornerback Christopher Owens.

39. IN THE 1960S, JOHN F. KENNEDY AND HIS BROTHERS VERY NEARLY PURCHASED THE PHILADELPHIA EAGLES FOR $6 MILLION.

40. WHILE THE NFL HAS NEVER HAD A FEMALE PLAYER, PATRICIA PALINKAS BECAME THE FIRST WOMAN TO PLAY PROFESSIONAL FOOTBALL ALL THE WAY BACK IN 1970, WHEN SHE SUITED UP FOR THE ATLANTIC COAST FOOTBALL LEAGUE'S ORLANDO PANTHERS.

41. WHILE PLAYING FOR NOTRE DAME, FUTURE NFL MVP JOE THEISMANN WAS CONVINCED TO CHANGE THE PRONUNCIATION OF HIS NAME FROM "THEES-MAN" TO "THIGHS-MAN" SPECIFICALLY SO IT WOULD RHYME WITH HEISMAN.

The gambit ultimately did not pay off, as he never won the Heisman.

42. AFTER THE AFL AND NFL MERGED IN 1970, THE NFC TEAMS COULD NOT AGREE ON A REALIGNMENT PLAN, SO IT WAS ULTIMATELY DETERMINED BY PICKING ONE OF THE FIVE OPTIONS ON THE TABLE OUT OF A HAT.

43. IN 1962, CBS MADE THE FIRST EXCLUSIVE RIGHTS DEAL TO BROADCAST NFL GAMES FOR JUST $4.65 MILLION. IN 2021, THE NFL'S DEALS WITH CBS, FOX, NBC, ESPN, AND AMAZON ARE WORTH A COLLECTIVE $110 BILLION.

44. THE SEVENTH PICK IN THE NFL DRAFT WAS NAMED "JOSH ALLEN" TWO YEARS IN A ROW.

In 2018, the Bills chose Wyoming quarterback Josh Allen, and in 2019, the Jaguars chose Kentucky linebacker Josh Allen.

45. THE BALTIMORE RAVENS WON THE 2000 SUPER BOWL DESPITE THE FACT THAT AT ONE POINT DURING THE SEASON THEY WENT FIVE STRAIGHT WEEKS WITHOUT SCORING A TOUCHDOWN. (THANKS TO ONE OF THE GREATEST DEFENSES OF ALL TIME, THEY STILL WENT 2-3 OVER THAT STRETCH.)

46. FOOTBALL HAS BEEN GROWING MORE POPULAR AMONG WOMEN FOR YEARS...BUT ONE STUDY SHOWED THAT POP ICON TAYLOR SWIFT'S RELATIONSHIP WITH KANSAS CITY CHIEFS TIGHT END TRAVIS KELCE SINGLEHANDEDLY SPIKED INTEREST BY MORE THAN 10%!

• 47 •

CHIEFS QUARTERBACK ELVIS GRBAC WAS ACCIDENTALLY NAMED PEOPLE MAGAZINE'S "SEXIEST ATHLETE ALIVE"

when a photographer sent to take pictures of "the Chiefs quarterback" failed to realize it was Grbac's backup, Rich Gannon, he had been sent to profile.

· 48 ·

IN 1997, KICKER
LIZ HEASTON BECAME
THE FIRST WOMAN TO
SCORE IN A COLLEGE
FOOTBALL GAME WHEN
SHE SUCCESSFULLY
KICKED AN EXTRA
POINT FOR WILLAMETTE
UNIVERSITY.

49. IN 2010, THE SAN DIEGO CHARGERS HAD THE #1 RANKED OFFENSE AND THE #1 RANKED DEFENSE... BUT SOMEHOW MISSED THE PLAYOFFS, THANKS TO A SPECIAL TEAMS UNIT THAT RANKED DEAD LAST IN THE LEAGUE.

50. HALL OF FAME 49ERS SAFETY RONNIE LOTT ONCE CHOSE TO HAVE PART OF HIS FINGER AMPUTATED IN ORDER TO AVOID A LENGTHY RECOVERY PROCESS AFTER BREAKING IT.
While the story is often cited to prove the toughness of NFL players, Lott himself has been vocal about regretting the decision.

51. IF A PUNT RETURNER CALLS FOR A FAIR CATCH, THEIR TEAM CAN IMMEDIATELY ATTEMPT AN UNCONTESTED FIELD GOAL FROM THE SPOT WHERE THE BALL WAS CAUGHT.
It's an odd rule that has only been invoked a handful of times in the history of the NFL.

52. THE OLDEST FOOTBALL TEAM IN NORTH AMERICA ISN'T THE BEARS OR CARDINALS, BUT THE CANADIAN FOOTBALL LEAGUE'S TORONTO ARGONAUTS.
The team was founded all the way back in 1873.

53. HOW DOMINANT WAS TOM BRADY'S LEGENDARY CAREER? OVER HIS 23 YEARS IN THE NFL, BRADY NEVER TOOK A SINGLE SNAP WITH HIS TEAM MATHEMATICALLY ELIMINATED FROM PLAYOFF CONTENTION.

54. WHILE A FEMALE NFL PLAYER MAY STILL BE A LONG WAY OFF, WOMEN HAVE HAD MORE SUCCESS BREAKING INTO THE WORLD OF OFFICIATING.
Sarah Thomas became the league's first female on-field official in 2019, and she was followed by Maia Chaka and Robin DeLorenzo in subsequent years. More to come, surely!

55. IN 2023, HALEY VAN VOORHIS BECAME THE FIRST WOMAN TO APPEAR IN AN NCAA FOOTBALL GAME AT A NON-KICKING POSITION.
She played safety for Division-III Shenandoah University.

56. THE NFL HAS NOT ALWAYS BEEN FRIENDLY TO WOMEN'S LEAGUES. IN 2002, THE NFL EFFECTIVELY FORCED THE NATIONAL WOMEN'S FOOTBALL LEAGUE TO CHANGE ITS NAME TO THE NATIONAL WOMEN'S FOOTBALL ASSOCIATION TO AVOID CONFUSION WITH THE NFL BRAND.
It also pressured the league to change team logos it deemed too similar to NFL logos. Not exactly the ally women's leagues might like.

57. IN 2001, COWBOYS GUARD NATE NEWTON WAS PULLED OVER WITH MARIJUANA IN HIS CAR...213 POUNDS OF MARIJUANA.

Just five weeks later, he was pulled over again...this time with 175 pounds of marijuana in his car.

58. IN 1999, BROWNS TACKLE ORLANDO BROWN WAS HIT IN THE EYE BY AN OFFICIAL'S PENALTY FLAG.

It temporarily blinded him in that eye and caused permanent damage that effectively ended his NFL career.

59. BENGALS SAFETY MIKE REID IS IN BOTH THE COLLEGE FOOTBALL HALL OF FAME...AND THE NASHVILLE SONGWRITERS HALL OF FAME.

Following his NFL career, Reid became an incredibly prolific songwriter.

60. LONGTIME NFL LONG SNAPPER JON DORENBOS BECAME A SUCCESSFUL MAGICIAN AFTER HIS PLAYING CAREER.

Dorenbos competed in the 11th season of *America's Got Talent* and finished in third place.

61. TRUE OR FALSE: THOUSANDS OF PEOPLE WERE GATHERING TO WATCH WOMEN PLAY FOOTBALL AS FAR BACK AS THE 1930S.

TRUE. Crowds of thousands gathered in Southern California to watch the so-called "girl gridders" showcase their skills for teams like the Star, Amazons, and Rinky Dinks.

62. TRUE OR FALSE: LEGENDARY VIKINGS DEFENSIVE LINEMAN ALAN PAGE WOULD LATER GO ON TO BECOME GOVERNOR OF MINNESOTA.

FALSE. He may not have become governor, but Page did go on to become a Minnesota Supreme Court Justice. During his playing days, Page was known for being active within the players' union.

63. TRUE OR FALSE: WONDERFUL TERRIFIC MONDS EARNED THE NICKNAME "WONDERFUL TERRIFIC" WHEN HIS COLLEGE TEAMMATES MADE FUN OF HIM FOR OVERUSING THOSE WORDS.

FALSE. Nope. Wonderful Terrific Monds is his real name! In fact, the former 49ers defensive back is Wonderful Terrific Monds, Jr., named after his father.

64. TRUE OR FALSE: WASHINGTON QUARTERBACK GUS FREROTTE ONCE INJURED HIMSELF BY PUNCHING A WALL WITH HIS THROWING HAND AFTER SCORING A TOUCHDOWN.

FALSE. In fact, he headbutted the wall in celebration and suffered a concussion and neck sprain.

65. TRUE OR FALSE: BENGALS WIDE RECEIVER CHAD JOHNSON LEGALLY CHANGED HIS NAME TO "CHAD OCHOCINCO."

TRUE. Johnson was so well known for wearing the number 85 throughout his career that he eventually made it official.

• 66 •

TRUE OR FALSE: TWO-TIME PRO BOWL CORNERBACK VONTAE DAVIS RETIRED IN THE MIDDLE OF A GAME.

TRUE. Davis was playing for the Bills in 2018 when he took himself out of the game and announced his retirement at halftime.

67. TRUE OR FALSE: STEELERS SAFETY TROY POLAMALU INSURED HIS FAMOUSLY LONG HAIR FOR $1 MILLION.

TRUE. Amazingly, this is true. Polamalu's image was synonymous with his hair, so it makes sense that he would want to protect it.

68. TRUE OR FALSE: UNTIL 1993, EACH NFL TEAM HAD TWO BYE WEEKS.

FALSE. Actually, 1993 is the only year in history that the NFL experimented with two bye weeks. It has never been done before or since.

69. TRUE OR FALSE: NO FEMALE PLAYER HAS EVER RECEIVED A FULL COLLEGE FOOTBALL SCHOLARSHIP.

FALSE. In 2018, defensive back Toni Harris became the first woman to receive a full college football scholarship, to play a non-kicking position when she committed to Central Methodist University.

70. TRUE OR FALSE: TIM TEBOW IS THE ONLY QUARTERBACK DRAFTED BY THE BRONCOS WHO HAS WON A PLAYOFF GAME FOR THE TEAM.

TRUE. Most of the Broncos most successful quarterbacks were drafted by other teams: John Elway and Peyton Manning were both drafted by the Colts, while Jake Plummer was drafted by the Cardinals.

71. **TRUE OR FALSE: FRANCO HARRIS'S FAMOUS "IMMACULATE RECEPTION" WAS THE VERY FIRST TOUCHDOWN THE STEELERS EVER SCORED IN THE PLAYOFFS.**

TRUE. The Steelers had only ever played one prior playoff game, and they were shut out in that matchup.

72. **TRUE OR FALSE: LEGENDARY COACH VINCE LOMBARDI NEVER LOST A SINGLE PLAYOFF GAME DURING HIS COACHING CAREER.**

FALSE. But not by much. The 1960 Philadelphia Eagles were the only team to ever defeat Lombardi in the playoffs.

73. **TRUE OR FALSE: A FAN WAS ONCE KILLED BY A FLYING LAWNMOWER AT AN NFL GAME.**

TRUE. Well, sort of—during a halftime show, a model airplane shaped like a lawnmower flew out of control and struck a fan, tragically killing him.

74. **TRUE OR FALSE: NO US-BASED TEAM HAS EVER WON THE CANADIAN FOOTBALL LEAGUE'S GREY CUP.**

FALSE. The Baltimore Stallions won the Grey Cup in 1995, becoming the only US team to be crowned CFL champions. Unfortunately for the Stallions, the team was relocated to Montreal the next year and became the latest incarnation of the Alouettes.

• 75 •

TRUE OR FALSE: TEDDY ROOSEVELT HATED FOOTBALL SO MUCH HE THREATENED TO BAN IT DURING HIS PRESIDENCY.

FALSE. While he did threaten to ban it, it wasn't out of personal distaste. In fact, Roosevelt probably saved the sport. It had grown so violent in the early 1900s that he threatened to ban it via executive order if the league didn't agree to make significant improvements to player safety.

[Baseball]

"Take me out to the ball game, take me out to the crowd…" These words are familiar to anyone who has ever attended a baseball game, but did you know the two men who wrote it had never been to a game themselves? Professional baseball dates back to the mid-1800s, and baseball historians have done an impressively good job documenting the game. That means there is no shortage of interesting facts, stories, and tidbits from not just today's game, but its early days as well. Whether you're talking about Rube Waddell, the legendary pitcher who had a habit of chasing fire trucks, or the pitcher who finished the game after being struck by lightning, America's pastime is full of fascinating tales!

1. **IN 1973, A PAIR OF NEW YORK YANKEES PLAYERS SWAPPED LIVES.**

   Yes, lives. They traded their wives, children, and even dogs, with each simply taking over where the other left off.

2. **NEITHER OF THE WRITERS OF "TAKE ME OUT TO THE BALL GAME" HAD EVER SEEN A GAME OF BASEBALL WHEN THEY WROTE THE SONG.**

3. **HALL OF FAMER STAN MUSIAL HAS THE FOURTH-MOST HITS IN MLB HISTORY WITH 3,630.**

   What makes that number more remarkable is that he collected exactly half of those hits at home and half on the road.

4. **WHEN PITTSBURGH PIRATES HALL OF FAME OUTFIELDER ROBERTO CLEMENTE WAS KILLED IN A PLANE CRASH WHILE CARRYING RELIEF SUPPLIES TO NICARAGUAN EARTHQUAKE VICTIMS, HE HAD EXACTLY 3,000 CAREER HITS.**

5. **IN THE 1890S, A NEW YORK STATE REPRESENTATIVE INTRODUCED A BILL ATTEMPTING TO BAN WOMEN FROM PLAYING BASEBALL.**

   Fortunately, his fellow legislators found the bill so ridiculous that they added a number of absurd provisions (including a stipulation that the ban only applied to red-headed women and an enforcement date more than a century in the future) before promptly killing it in committee.

6. **THE NEW YORK YANKEES WENT AN ASTONISHING 308 GAMES WITHOUT BEING SHUT OUT FROM 1931 TO 1933.**

That's almost 100 games more than the second-longest streak, which is owned by (you guessed it) the New York Yankees.

7. **IN 2001, ARIZONA DIAMONDBACKS PITCHER RANDY JOHNSON ACCIDENTALLY HIT A BIRD WITH A 100 MPH FASTBALL. IT DID NOT END WELL FOR THE BIRD, AND JOHNSON WAS HORRIFIED.**

8. **IN 1974, CLEVELAND'S BASEBALL TEAM HOSTED A 10¢ BEER NIGHT THAT LED TO A CROWD SO BELLIGERENTLY DRUNK THAT THE UMPIRES WERE EVENTUALLY FORCED TO FORFEIT THE GAME TO CLEVELAND'S OPPONENT.**

Predictably, this led to a riot.

9. **MLB UMPIRES ARE REQUIRED BY RULE TO WEAR BLACK UNDERWEAR...JUST IN CASE THEY SPLIT THEIR BLACK PANTS.**

10. **OF THE MLB PITCHERS IN THE ALL-TIME TOP TEN FOR CAREER WINS, ONLY THREE WERE BORN AFTER 1900.**

Two were born before the Civil War ended!

11. **THE AVERAGE LIFESPAN OF AN MLB BASEBALL IS JUST SEVEN PITCHES.**

· 12 ·

IN 1993, A FLY BALL HIT TEXAS RANGERS OUTFIELDER JOSE CANSECO ON THE HEAD AND BOUNCED OVER THE WALL FOR A HOME RUN.

· 13 ·

METS MANAGER BOBBY VALENTINE WAS ONCE EJECTED FROM A GAME, BUT RETURNED TO THE DUGOUT WEARING A "DISGUISE" CONSISTING OF A FAKE MUSTACHE AND STREET CLOTHES.

14. FOUR PLAYERS IN MLB HISTORY HAVE BEEN TRADED FOR THEMSELVES (TECHNICALLY, EACH FULFILLED THE "PLAYER TO BE NAMED LATER" CONSIDERATION IN THEIR RESPECTIVE TRADES).

15. IN 1920, BABE RUTH HIT 54 HOME RUNS. NO OTHER TEAM IN THE AMERICAN LEAGUE THAT YEAR HIT THAT MANY HOME RUNS...TOTAL.

16. CINCINNATI REDS OWNER MARGE SCHOTT WAS BANNED FROM MANAGING THE TEAM FOR THREE YEARS AFTER MAKING SYMPATHETIC COMMENTS ABOUT ADOLF HITLER.

She was pressured to sell the team shortly thereafter.

17. IN 1970, PIRATES PITCHER DOCK ELLIS THREW A NO-HITTER AGAINST THE PADRES. WHAT MAKES THIS NO-HITTER PARTICULARLY REMARKABLE IS THE FACT THAT HE WAS REPORTEDLY UNDER THE EFFECTS OF LSD THE ENTIRE TIME.

18. IN 1917, RED SOX PITCHER ERNIE SHORE PITCHED AN UNOFFICIAL PERFECT GAME.

Why unofficial? Shore was on the mound for 27 consecutive outs...but only after the game's starting pitcher, Babe Ruth, walked the first batter and was ejected for punching the umpire.

19. IN 1985, AN APRIL FOOLS' DAY JOKE WENT VIRAL AND LED MULTIPLE MLB TEAMS TO BELIEVE THAT A FICTIONAL PITCHER NAMED SIDD FINCH WAS A REAL PROSPECT CAPABLE OF THROWING 168 MPH FASTBALLS AFTER STUDYING WITH YOGA INSTRUCTORS IN TIBET.

20. PITCHER OLD HOSS RADBOURN HOLDS THE RECORD FOR MOST WINS IN A SEASON, WITH 60 IN 1884.

Only two other pitchers have eclipsed 50 wins in a season, and only a small handful of pitchers have even won 30 games since 1900.

21. LIZZIE MURPHY, KNOWN AS "THE QUEEN OF BASEBALL," BECAME ONE OF THE FIRST WOMEN TO PLAY PROFESSIONAL BASEBALL IN 1922.

She was an incredible self-promoter, wearing a customized jersey with her name on the front so fans could identify her from the stands. She remains the only woman to have played for a major league team in a major league ballpark.

22. DURING THE NINTH INNING OF A 1919 GAME, CLEVELAND PITCHER RAY CALDWELL WAS STRUCK BY LIGHTNING AND KNOCKED UNCONSCIOUS FOR SEVERAL MINUTES.

Upon waking up, he waved off his manager and stayed in the game to record the final out.

• 23 •

AFTER DISGUISING HERSELF AS A BOY, KATHRYN JOHNSTON BECAME THE FIRST GIRL TO PLAY LITTLE LEAGUE BASEBALL IN 1951.

Her coach allowed her to continue playing even after discovering the truth, but Little League Baseball officially banned girls from play the following year, a rule that lasted until a 1974 lawsuit granted girls the right to play.

• 24 •

RUBE WADDELL WAS ONE OF THE GREATEST PITCHERS IN THE HISTORY OF BASEBALL.

He was also extremely eccentric; he was easily distracted by things like puppies and shiny objects, and on multiple occasions left the field during a game to chase a passing fire truck.

25. THE SHORTEST PLAYER TO EVER APPEAR IN A MAJOR LEAGUE BASEBALL GAME WAS EDDIE GAEDEL, WHO STOOD 3 FEET, 7 INCHES TALL.

He was signed by the St. Louis Browns as a publicity stunt, and wore the jersey number "1/8" during his lone game.

26. RELIEF PITCHER TURK WENDELL, WHO PLAYED FOR SEVERAL TEAMS BETWEEN 1993 AND 2004, WAS KNOWN FOR BRUSHING HIS TEETH BETWEEN EVERY INNING OF PLAY.

He was even featured on a baseball card brushing his teeth.

27. OVER THE YEARS, A SIGNIFICANT NUMBER OF BASEBALL PLAYERS HAVE ADMITTED TO AN UNCONVENTIONAL METHOD OF TOUGHENING THEIR HANDS: THEY URINATE ON THEM.

28. IN 1985, THERE WAS A MASSIVE DRUG SCANDAL IN BASEBALL, AND THE PIRATES MASCOT WAS DISCOVERED TO HAVE BEEN DEALING COCAINE... SOMETIMES TO THE TEAM'S OWN PLAYERS.

29. GAME 6 OF THE 1986 WORLD SERIES IS BEST KNOWN AS THE GAME WHEN BILL BUCKNER LET A GROUND BALL ROLL THROUGH HIS LEGS. IT OVERSHADOWED SOMETHING EVEN MORE SHOCKING: A FAN PARACHUTED ONTO THE FIELD DURING THE GAME WEARING A SIGN THAT SAID, "GO METS!"

30. AMAZINGLY, LIZZIE MURPHY (THE AFOREMENTIONED "QUEEN OF BASEBALL") WAS ALSO THE FIRST BASEBALL PLAYER—OF EITHER GENDER—TO PLAY FOR BOTH AN AMERICAN LEAGUE TEAM AND A NATIONAL LEAGUE TEAM.

Murphy even suited up for a Negro League team, becoming the first woman to play in that league as well.

31. COLORADO ROCKIES HALL OF FAMER TODD HELTON WAS A TWO-SPORT STAR IN COLLEGE. IN FACT, HE WAS THE STARTING QUARTERBACK FOR THE UNIVERSITY OF TENNESSEE FOOTBALL TEAM, AHEAD OF FUTURE HALL OF FAMER PEYTON MANNING!

32. BASEBALL LEGEND TY COBB WAS ONCE SUSPENDED FOR JUMPING INTO THE STANDS AND ASSAULTING A FAN WHO HAD BEEN HECKLING HIM ALL GAME.

The fan was a disabled man with no hands, so taunting the notoriously violent and short-tempered Cobb may not have been the best decision.

33. DODGERS OUTFIELDER FERNANDO TATÍS SR. IS THE ONLY PLAYER IN MLB HISTORY TO HIT TWO GRAND SLAMS IN THE SAME INNING.

34. IN 1933, PITCHER CLARENCE BLETHEN SLID INTO SECOND BASE WITH HIS FALSE TEETH IN HIS BACK POCKET. THE TEETH CLAMPED DOWN AND TOOK A CHUNK OUT OF HIS REAR END, FORCING HIM TO EXIT THE GAME.

· 35 ·

PITCHER "DOC" MEDICH EARNED HIS NICKNAME BECAUSE HE COMPLETED HIS MEDICAL DEGREE DURING HIS BASEBALL CAREER.

It's a good thing, too: not once, but twice Doc made his way into the stands to render assistance to a fan suffering a heart attack.

Connie MORGAN

Mamie JOHNSON

Toni STONE

• 36 •

WHILE WOMEN HAVEN'T HAD MUCH LUCK WITH MAJOR LEAGUE BASEBALL, A SURPRISING NUMBER OF WOMEN SUITED UP FOR NEGRO LEAGUE TEAMS IN THE 1950S.

Toni Stone, Mamie Johnson, and Connie Morgan all made history in the Negro leagues, where they overcame significant prejudice and discrimination to make their mark on the game.

37. TONI STONE HAS A PARTICULARLY INTERESTING HISTORICAL CONNECTION: SHE GOT HER CHANCE TO PLAY IN THE NEGRO LEAGUES WHEN SHE WAS CALLED UPON TO REPLACE FUTURE HOME RUN KING HANK AARON, WHO HAD LEFT TO PLAY IN MAJOR LEAGUE BASEBALL.

38. FORFEITED GAMES ARE INCREDIBLY RARE IN MODERN BASEBALL. THE MOST RECENT FORFEIT HAPPENED IN 1995, WHEN DODGERS FANS DISRUPTED A GAME AGAINST THE CARDINALS BY REPEATEDLY THROWING SOUVENIR BASEBALLS ONTO THE FIELD.

39. IN 1976, TWO PROTESTERS RAN ONTO THE FIELD AT DODGER STADIUM, PLANNING TO LIGHT AN AMERICAN FLAG ON FIRE.

That didn't sit well with Dodgers outfielder Rick Monday, who raced over to the duo and snatched the flag away before they could strike the match.

40. JACKIE MITCHELL ONCE STRUCK OUT BABE RUTH AND LOU GEHRIG DURING A MINOR LEAGUE EXHIBITION GAME. WHAT MAKES THAT SO SPECIAL?

Well, Jackie Mitchell was a teenage girl—and one of the first women to ever suit up for a professional baseball game.

41. ONLY ONE PITCHER HAS THROWN A PERFECT GAME IN THE PLAYOFFS. IN GAME 5 OF THE 1956 WORLD SERIES, YANKEES STARTER DON LARSEN ACCOMPLISHED THE FEAT BY BLANKING THE BROOKLYN DODGERS.

42. IN 2014, 17-YEAR-OLD CHELSEA BAKER THREW BATTING PRACTICE PITCHES FOR THE TAMPA BAY RAYS. KNOWN FOR HER ABSOLUTELY VICIOUS KNUCKLEBALL, BAKER MADE MULTIPLE PROFESSIONAL PLAYERS LOOK FOOLISH.

Baker's command of the famously hard-to-hit pitch was so great that she once threw two perfect games in one year for her Little League team!

43. YOU'VE HEARD OF THE CURSE OF THE BAMBINO, BUT HOW ABOUT THE CURSE OF THE COLONEL?

Japan's Hansin Tigers baseball team was reportedly "cursed" by the KFC founder and mascot after a statue of the Colonel was tossed in the river by a fan celebrating the team's 1985 championship win. The team endured an 18-year streak of futility following the incident and has not won a championship since.

44. THE FIRST (AND SO FAR ONLY) WOMAN TO BE ELECTED TO THE MLB HALL OF FAME WAS EFFA MANLEY.

While it might be unexpected for a Negro league owner to make the Hall of Fame, Manley was a tireless advocate for civil rights and became known for working to improve conditions for her players.

• 45 •

CLEVELAND RELIEF PITCHER JASON GRIMSLEY ONCE CRAWLED THROUGH THE CEILING TO ACCESS A LOCKED UMPIRE'S ROOM TO SWAP OUT A CORKED BAT BEFORE IT COULD BE TESTED.

He managed to successfully swap the bats...but didn't cover his tracks particularly well.

• 46 •

TWINS OUTFIELDER
DENARD SPAN ONCE
HIT HIS OWN MOTHER
IN THE STANDS WITH
A FOUL BALL.

47. SIMILAR TO THE SPAN INCIDENT, CLEVELAND PITCHER BOB FELLER ONCE THREW A PITCH THAT WAS FOULED OFF BY THE BATTER AND HIT HIS MOTHER.

The kicker? It happened on Mother's Day!

48. IN 2008, CC SABATHIA BECAME THE ONLY PLAYER IN MLB HISTORY TO LEAD BOTH THE AL AND NL IN COMPLETE-GAME SHUTOUTS IN THE SAME SEASON.

He had two shutouts with Cleveland before being traded to the Brewers—good enough for the lead in both leagues.

49. ATLANTA SECOND BASEMAN MARK LEMKE HOLDS THE RECORD FOR MOST MLB PLATE APPEARANCES WITHOUT EVER BEING HIT BY A PITCH. HE STEPPED UP TO THE PLATE 3,664 TIMES AND WAS NEVER PLUNKED.

For context, Ozzie Albies, Atlanta's starting second baseman in 2023, was hit by eight pitches that year alone!

50. SAMMY SOSA IS THE ONLY PLAYER IN HISTORY TO HIT 60 OR MORE HOME RUNS IN A SEASON THREE TIMES.

Unluckily for Sosa, he did not lead the league in homers during any of those seasons. His 66 homers in 1998 were four short of Mark McGwire's 70, his 64 homers in 2001 fell short of Barry Bonds' 73, and his 63 in 1999 were again short of McGwire's 65.

51. GREG MADDUX WAS SUCH AN EFFICIENT PITCHER THAT THERE IS AN UNOFFICIAL STATISTIC NAMED AFTER HIM TODAY: A "MADDUX" REFERS TO THROWING A COMPLETE-GAME SHUTOUT WITH LESS THAN 100 PITCHES.

52. AS OF THIS PUBLICATION, KIM NG IS THE ONLY WOMAN TO EVER HOLD A GENERAL MANAGER POSITION IN ANY OF THE FOUR MAJOR NORTH AMERICAN SPORTS.

She served as the general manager of MLB's Miami Marlins from 2021 to 2023, during which time she helmed the team to an unexpected playoff appearance.

53. AMID A SCANDAL-RIDDLED 1899 SEASON IN WHICH THE TEAM'S OWNERSHIP UNDERMINED THE TEAM IN A NUMBER OF WAYS, THE CLEVELAND SPIDERS BECAME THE WORST TEAM IN MLB HISTORY, WITH AN UNFATHOMABLY BAD RECORD OF 20-134.

54. WOMEN WERE TECHNICALLY BARRED FROM PLAYING MAJOR LEAGUE BASEBALL FROM 1952 TO 1992.

Despite the ban being lifted, no woman has since played in the majors. Hopefully it's just a matter of time!

55. PERHAPS THE FUNNIEST COMBINATION OF NAME AND NICKNAME BELONGS TO LEFT FIELDER JOHNNY DICKSHOT, WHO WENT BY THE MONIKER "UGLY DICKSHOT" FOR MUCH OF HIS CAREER.

56. CECIL FIELDER AND PRINCE FIELDER ARE ONE OF THE FEW FATHER AND SON DUOS TO PLAY IN THE MLB.

Amazingly, they both ended their careers with exactly 319 home runs.

57. IN 1898, LIZZIE ARLINGTON BECAME THE FIRST WOMAN TO PLAY FOR A PROFESSIONAL MEN'S BASEBALL TEAM WHEN SHE SIGNED WITH THE MINOR LEAGUE READING COAL HEAVERS.

She pitched the 9th inning of a game against the Allentown Peanuts, preserving the win for her side.

58. IN 2009, PITCHER ERI YOSHIDA BECAME THE FIRST WOMAN TO PLAY PROFESSIONAL BASEBALL IN TWO DIFFERENT COUNTRIES.

She became the first woman drafted by a Japanese men's professional baseball team in 2008 before agreeing to play in the US's Arizona Fall League the following year.

59. IN 2018, A RED SOX FAN THREW BACK A HOME RUN HIT BY YANKEES SLUGGER GIANCARLO STANTON AND ACCIDENTALLY HIT STANTON WITH IT AS HE ROUNDED SECOND BASE.

Stanton had a sense of humor about it and tipped his helmet to the fan.

60. IN 1929, DALLAS STEERS PITCHER "OYSTER JOE" MARTINA NEGOTIATED HIS RELEASE FROM THE TEAM IN EXCHANGE FOR TWO BARRELS OF OYSTERS.

Funnily enough, he was already known as "Oyster Joe" prior to the incident. (He was the son of a prominent oyster dealer.)

61. TRUE OR FALSE: LEGENDARY HITTER TONY GWYNN HAD FOUR HITS IN A GAME MORE TIMES THAN HE HAD TWO STRIKEOUTS IN A GAME.

TRUE. Amazing, it's true. Gwynn was one of the most disciplined hitters in modern MLB history.

62. TRUE OR FALSE: ACCORDING TO THE MLB, CATCHING A BALL IN YOUR HAT IS TECHNICALLY ILLEGAL.

TRUE. To be considered a catch, the ball must be caught using a hand or glove.

63. TRUE OR FALSE: NO PLAYER HAS EVER BEEN TRADED IN THE MIDDLE OF A DOUBLEHEADER.

FALSE. Way back in 1922, the Cubs and Cardinals swapped outfielders Max Flack and Cliff Heathcote after game one of their doubleheader. Both players suited up for their new teams and started game two.

64. TRUE OR FALSE: MLB LOWERED THE HEIGHT OF THE PITCHER'S MOUND IN RESPONSE TO ONE PITCHER'S DOMINANT PLAY.

TRUE. Hall of Fame pitcher Bob Gibson was so dominant during the 1968 season that it prompted MLB to permanently lower the mound by five inches to give pitchers less of an advantage.

65. TRUE OR FALSE: HOYT WILHELM HOLDS THE RECORD FOR THE MOST HOME RUNS BY AN MLB PITCHER.

FALSE. But Wilhelm is notable for another reason: he hit a home run in his very first MLB at bat, then never hit another for the rest of his career.

· 66 ·

TRUE OR FALSE: THE MOVIE *A LEAGUE OF THEIR OWN* IS BASED ON A TRUE STORY.

TRUE. During World War II, the All-American Girls Professional Baseball League was founded, with teams of women traveling around the country to entertain fans while many of the era's most famous athletes were fighting in the war. The league lasted from 1943 to 1954 and would later be memorialized in the film *A League of Their Own*.

67. TRUE OR FALSE: A FAN WAS ONCE INJURED BY TWO FOUL BALLS ON CONSECUTIVE PITCHES.

TRUE. In 1957, Phillies outfielder Richie Ashburn struck a fan with a foul ball, breaking her nose. After a brief stoppage to provide medical attention to the fan, Ashburn hit the very next pitch directly at her once again, this time breaking a bone in her leg as she was being carried out on a stretcher.

68. TRUE OR FALSE: THERE HAS NEVER BEEN A FEMALE ON-FIELD COACH IN MLB HISTORY.

FALSE. Alyssa Nakken became the first woman to officially serve as an on-field coach in 2022, taking the place of San Francisco Giants first base coach Antoan Richardson after he was ejected for arguing with an opposing coach.

69. TRUE OR FALSE: DURING WWII, THE AMERICAN MILITARY INTENTIONALLY DESIGNED HAND GRENADES TO BE THE APPROXIMATE SIZE AND SHAPE OF A BASEBALL.

TRUE. The military (correctly, it seems) reasoned that since just about any kid in America could throw a baseball, designing grenades to mimic them would ensure soldiers could throw them with ease.

70. TRUE OR FALSE: THE FIRST OFFICIAL WOMEN'S BASEBALL TEAM WAS FORMED IN 1939.

FALSE. Women are not new to baseball—in fact, Vassar College started the first women's baseball team all the way back in 1866.

71. TRUE OR FALSE: THE PHILLIE PHANATIC ONCE GOT INTO A PHYSICAL ALTERCATION WITH AN OPPOSING MANAGER.

TRUE. Yes, Dodgers manager Tommy Lasorda was a legend for his play...but also for his temper. One day, he had simply had enough of the Phanatic's antics.

72. TRUE OR FALSE: THE YEAR HE HIT 61 HOME RUNS, ROGER MARIS ALSO SET THE RECORD (AT THE TIME) FOR INTENTIONAL WALKS.

FALSE. In fact, Maris was not intentionally walked a single time during his record-setting season. Of course, that probably had something to do with the fact that he was hitting ahead of Mickey Mantle.

73. TRUE OR FALSE: THERE IS EXACTLY ONE WOMAN IN THE MLB HALL OF FAME.

TRUE. Effa Manley was the co-owner of the Newark Eagles of the Negro National League, and was inducted into the Hall of Fame in 2006 in recognition of her efforts on behalf of Black players.

74. TRUE OR FALSE: THE RED SOX SOLD BABE RUTH TO THE YANKEES TO FINANCE A BROADWAY PLAY.

FALSE. It has become a popular myth that Ruth was sold to help team owner Harry Frazee finance the play *No, No Nanette*, but historians broadly agree that this is unlikely.

• 75 •

TRUE OR FALSE: RED SOX FANS ONCE STAGED AN EXORCISM AT FENWAY PARK.

TRUE. The fans were desperate to break the "Curse of the Bambino," and were willing to try just about anything.

{ Basketball]

Basketball has some of the most impressive individual accomplishments in any sport: Wilt Chamberlain scoring 100 points in a game is a feat that will probably never be matched, let alone topped. But it also has some of the most fascinating oddities. Did you know slam dunks used to be banned in college basketball? Or that shattering a backboard is officially a technical foul? Did you know that the NBA once had a player with no ACLs...and a player with extra ACLs? Basketball is a game known for its bombastic personalities, amazing performances, and unmatched entertainment value.

1. JAMES NAISMITH IS THE ONLY COACH IN THE HISTORY OF THE UNIVERSITY OF KANSAS MEN'S BASKETBALL PROGRAM WITH A LOSING RECORD... WHICH IS IRONIC, SINCE HE INVENTED THE SPORT.

2. DESPITE BEING FOUNDED IN 1898, THE KANSAS MEN'S BASKETBALL PROGRAM HAS ONLY HAD EIGHT HEAD COACHES. TOTAL.

3. ANDRE DRUMMOND HOLDS THE RECORD FOR THE MOST MISSED FREE THROWS IN A SINGLE GAME, WITH 23 MISSES IN A GAME AGAINST THE HOUSTON ROCKETS IN 2016.

4. WHILE THE REFEREES TYPICALLY WAIVE IT OFF, IT IS OFFICIALLY A TECHNICAL FOUL TO SHATTER A BACKBOARD.

5. DURING THE 1961–62 SEASON, WILT CHAMBERLAIN AVERAGED 48.5 MINUTES PER GAME, DESPITE THE FACT THAT AN NBA GAME LASTS JUST 48 MINUTES. He played every minute of 79 games that season, including every overtime minute.

6. FROM 1990 TO 1998, THE CHICAGO BULLS NEVER LOST THREE GAMES IN A ROW WHILE MICHAEL JORDAN WAS ON THE TEAM.

7. THE SLAM DUNK WAS BANNED IN HIGH SCHOOL AND COLLEGE BASKETBALL FROM 1967 UNTIL 1976.

8. HALL OF FAME CENTER SHAQUILLE O'NEAL MADE EXACTLY ONE THREE-POINT SHOT IN HIS ENTIRE CAREER.

9. CELTICS LEGEND PAUL PIERCE WAS STABBED 11 TIMES JUST BEFORE THE START OF THE 2000-01 SEASON...BUT STILL MANAGED TO PLAY IN EVERY SINGLE GAME THAT YEAR.

10. BASKETBALL WAS ORIGINALLY PLAYED WITH NINE PLAYERS PER SIDE (THREE CENTERS, THREE FORWARDS, AND THREE BACKS). THIS WAS QUICKLY RECOGNIZED AS UNWIELDY AND LOWERED TO FIVE.

11. IN BASKETBALL'S EARLY DAYS, DRIBBLING WAS NOT ALLOWED. OFFENSIVE PLAYERS COULD NOT ADVANCE THE BALL THEMSELVES—THEY COULD ONLY PASS IT OR SHOOT IT.

Eventually, they were permitted a single dribble, before the game evolved to its current state.

12. WILT CHAMBERLAIN IS THE ONLY NBA PLAYER TO SCORE 100 POINTS IN A SINGLE GAME.

In a twist that delights conspiracy theorists everywhere, no video footage of that game exists.

• 13 •

WHEN KOBE BRYANT WAS DRAFTED BY THE LOS ANGELES LAKERS, HE HADN'T YET TURNED 18.

As a result, his first contract had to be cosigned by his parents.

• 14 •

DURING THE 1987-88 SEASON, THE TALLEST PLAYER IN THE HISTORY OF THE NBA (MANUTE BOL, 7'7") AND THE SHORTEST PLAYER IN THE HISTORY OF THE NBA (MUGGSY BOGUES, 5'3") PLAYED ON THE SAME TEAM.

15. MANUTE BOL IS THE ONLY PLAYER IN NBA HISTORY TO HAVE MORE BLOCKS THAN POINTS.

16. DESPITE BEING THE SHORTEST PLAYER IN NBA HISTORY, MUGGSY BOGUES STILL MANAGED TO BLOCK 39 SHOTS OVER THE COURSE OF HIS ILLUSTRIOUS CAREER.

17. MICHAEL JORDAN WAS NOT THE FIRST OVERALL PICK IN THE NBA DRAFT.

He went third, after Hakeem Olajuwon (a Hall of Famer in his own right) and Sam Bowie (a pick that Portland Trail Blazers fans lament to this day).

18. WHILE THEY ARE ALMOST ALWAYS REFERRED TO AS THE "KNICKS," THE NBA TEAM IN NEW YORK IS OFFICIALLY NAMED THE "KNICKERBOCKERS."

19. THE FIRST GAME IN THE HISTORY OF THE BASKETBALL ASSOCIATION OF AMERICA (BAA), THE PRECURSOR TO THE NBA, WAS PLAYED BETWEEN THE NEW YORK KNICKERBOCKERS AND THE TORONTO HUSKIES IN 1946.

The Huskies would disband the very next year, and Toronto would be without an NBA team until the Raptors were founded in 1995.

20. MICHAEL JORDAN'S ICONIC "AIR JORDAN" SNEAKERS WERE ORIGINALLY BANNED BY THE NBA FOR VIOLATING THE UNIFORM CODE.

21. AFTER LOSING TO THE ROCKETS IN THE 1995 NBA FINALS, THEN-ORLANDO MAGIC STAR SHAQUILLE O'NEAL WAS SO FURIOUS WITH ROCKETS STAR HAKEEM OLAJUWON THAT HE CHALLENGED HIM TO A ONE-ON-ONE MATCH.

Sadly, it never came to fruition.

22. THE CREATOR OF THE POPULAR VIDEO GAME *NBA JAM* WAS A DETROIT PISTONS FAN WHO HATED THE CHICAGO BULLS.

He hated them so much that, years later, he admitted to surreptitiously rigging the game to make the Bulls miss shots when they were playing the Pistons.

23. DURING BASKETBALL'S EARLIEST DAYS, A JUMP BALL WAS HELD AT CENTER COURT AFTER EVERY SINGLE BASKET.

As you can imagine, this made the pace of play glacial, and was quickly abandoned.

24. TWO WOMEN HAVE BEEN SELECTED IN THE NBA DRAFT.

Denise Long was selected by the San Francisco Warriors in 1969, although the league voided the pick. In 1977, the New Orleans Jazz chose Lusia Harris, and this time the league let it stand. Unfortunately, she was not interested in playing in the NBA and declined her invitation to the team's camp.

• 25 •

IN THE 1930S, A WOMEN'S TEAM CALLED THE ALL-AMERICAN RED HEADS TRAVELED AROUND THE COUNTRY TO PLAY AGAINST MEN'S TEAMS.

Where did the name come from? Well, to join the team, players were forced to either dye their hair or wear red wigs. Amazingly, this strange team was the very first professional women's basketball team.

• 26 •

THE HIGHEST-SCORING PLAYER IN THE HISTORY OF NCAA DIVISION-I BASKETBALL IS NOT A FUTURE NBA STAR, BUT IOWA POINT GUARD CAITLIN CLARK.

In 2024, she broke the scoring record that had been held by "Pistol" Pete Maravich for over 50 years.

27. WHILE CAITLIN CLARK MAY BE THE NEW NCAA SCORING LEADER, EVEN SHE CAN'T TOUCH PEARL MOORE'S RECORD.

Moore scored 4,061 points from 1975–79, but women's basketball was governed by the Association for Intercollegiate Athletics for Women (AIAW) at the time, rather than the NCAA.

28. DESPITE BEING BORN WITH A SEVERE HEARING IMPAIRMENT, INDIANA FEVER STAR TAMIKA CATCHINGS WAS NAMED 2002 WNBA ROOKIE OF THE YEAR AND WOULD GO ON TO MAKE TEN ALL-STAR TEAMS DURING HER STORIED CAREER!

29. FORMER NBA CENTER DEJUAN BLAIR PLAYED HIS ENTIRE CAREER WITHOUT AN ACL IN EITHER KNEE.

He wasn't aware of the missing ligaments himself until the year he was drafted!

30. ON THE OTHER SIDE OF THE EQUATION, THERE IS DENNIS SMITH JR. THE JOURNEYMAN POINT GUARD WAS BORN WITH AN EXTRA LIGAMENT IN HIS LEFT KNEE!

31. THE LONGEST WINNING STREAK IN COLLEGE BASKET-BALL HISTORY IS 111 WINS, RECORDED BY THE UCONN WOMEN'S BASKETBALL TEAM FROM 2014 TO 2017.

The streak ended with a loss to Mississippi State in the 2017 NCAA tournament, but the team's regular-season winning streak reached 126 straight wins before the team lost to Baylor in 2019.

32. ANN MEYERS DRYSDALE WAS THE FIRST WOMAN TO SIGN AN NBA CONTRACT, ALL THE WAY BACK IN 1979 WHEN SHE WAS PAID $50,000 TO TRY OUT FOR THE INDIANA PACERS.

She didn't make the team, but she did go on to play professional basketball in the Women's Professional Basketball League.

33. DURING HIS TIME AT UCLA, KAREEM ABDUL-JABBAR LOST JUST TWO GAMES WHILE WINNING THREE NCAA CHAMPIONSHIPS.

That means he was more likely to win the championship than lose a single game.

34. ONLY ONE BROADCASTER HAS EVER BEEN EJECTED FROM AN NBA GAME.

Portland Trail Blazers commentator Mike Rice was ejected from a game in 1994 for arguing with a referee.

35. IN 1994, THE NEW JERSEY NETS SERIOUSLY CONSIDERED CHANGING THEIR NAME TO THE NEW JERSEY SWAMP DRAGONS.

The proposal was overwhelmingly approved by the other NBA owners...only for the Nets to change their minds.

36. IN 1974, "PISTOL" PETE MARAVICH TOLD A REPORTER, "I DON'T WANT TO PLAY TEN YEARS IN THE NBA AND DIE OF A HEART ATTACK AT AGE 40."

Maravich went on to have a ten-year career in the NBA, and died of a heart attack at age 40.

• 37 •

KNICKS CENTER
MARCUS CAMBY WAS
ONCE SUSPENDED FOR
FIVE GAMES AFTER
TRYING TO PUNCH AN
OPPOSING PLAYER AND
ACCIDENTALLY HITTING
HIS OWN COACH
IN THE FACE.

• 38 •

IN 2009, TENNESSEE'S PAT SUMMITT BECAME THE FIRST COLLEGE BASKETBALL COACH IN HISTORY TO REACH 1,000 WINS.

She has since been joined by longtime Duke coach Mike Krzyzewski and Syracuse legend Jim Boeheim, but it was Summitt who blazed the trail.

39. IN 2018, THE WNBA'S LAS VEGAS ACES FORFEITED A GAME WHEN PLAYERS REFUSED TO TAKE THE COURT AFTER A NIGHTMARISH 25-HOUR TRAVEL EXPERIENCE.

It was the first game the WNBA was ever forced to cancel, but the team insisted that the experience had put its players at too great a risk of injury.

40. WOMEN'S COLLEGE BASKETBALL DIDN'T GET ITS OWN MARCH MADNESS EVENT UNTIL 1982, AND THE FINALISTS WEREN'T WHAT YOU MIGHT EXPECT.

While teams like UConn and Tennessee would come to dominate women's college basketball in subsequent years, the first-ever tournament final was played between Louisiana Tech and Cheyney State. Louisiana Tech was led by a player named Kim Mulkey, who (as of this publication) has won four NCAA women's basketball championships as a coach (three with Baylor and one with LSU).

41. THE RECORD FOR MOST MISSED THREE-POINTERS IN AN NBA GAME IS 16.

That record is a tie between Damon Stoudamire, who did it once, and James Harden...who, as of this writing, has done it six times.

42. THE DALLAS MAVERICKS ONCE HAD THREE PLAYERS WITH THE EXACT SAME BIRTHDATE.

Deron Williams, Raymond Felton, and J. J. Barea were all born on June 26, 1984. Even more amazingly, all three played the same position!

43. FAMOUSLY UNPOPULAR NBA REFEREE JOEY CRAWFORD WAS ONCE SUSPENDED INDEFINITELY AFTER ALLEGEDLY CHALLENGING SPURS HALL OF FAMER TIM DUNCAN TO A FIGHT IN THE MIDDLE OF A GAME.

44. AT THE BEGINNING OF THE RUSSIA-UKRAINE CONFLICT, WNBA STAR BRITTNEY GRINER WAS DETAINED IN RUSSIA FOR POSSESSION OF CANNABIS.

She was eventually returned to the US in a prisoner exchange involving Viktor Bout, a Russian arms dealer and inspiration for the Nicolas Cage film *Lord of War*.

45. IN 1954, THE NBA PLAYED AN EXPERIMENTAL GAME BETWEEN THE HAWKS AND LAKERS THAT FEATURED 12-FOOT RIMS.

The reason was that NBA executives were reportedly concerned the scoring had become "too easy" in the NBA.

46. ONLY THREE PLAYERS HAVE EVER WON THE NBA SCORING TITLE WHILE ALSO BEING NAMED TO THE NBA ALL-DEFENSIVE TEAM.

Jerry West did it once. Kobe Bryant did it twice. And Michael Jordan did it an incredible nine times.

47. THE FIRST PLAYER EVER SELECTED IN THE NBA DRAFT NEVER ACTUALLY PLAYED IN THE LEAGUE.

Clifton McNeely decided to become a high school basketball coach instead of playing in the NBA.

• 48 •

IN 1949, THE CELTICS SELECTED TONY LAVELLI FOURTH OVERALL IN THE NBA DRAFT, BUT HE INITIALLY REFUSED TO PLAY FOR THE TEAM BECAUSE HE WANTED TO ATTEND JUILLIARD FOR MUSIC.

Eventually, the Celtics convinced him to join the team on the condition that he could play his beloved accordion during halftime.

· 49 ·

CAVALIERS GUARD
J. R. SMITH WAS ONCE
SUSPENDED ONE GAME
FOR THROWING A
BOWL OF CHICKEN
TORTILLA SOUP AT AN
ASSISTANT COACH.

50. LEGENDARY SAN ANTONIO SPURS CENTER TIM DUNCAN PLAYED 19 YEARS IN THE NBA AND NEVER WON FEWER THAN 50 GAMES (EXCEPT IN THE STRIKE-SHORTENED 1998–99 SEASON).

51. DESPITE THE FACT THAT THERE ARE JUST 82 GAMES IN AN NBA SEASON, WALT BELLAMY PLAYED 88 GAMES DURING 1968–69.

This occurred because he was traded during the season, and the schedule was not as balanced as it is in today's NBA.

52. IN TERMS OF TIME SPENT ON THE COURT, JAMESON CURRY HOLDS THE RECORD FOR THE SHORTEST NBA CAREER.

In 2010, he played just 3.9 seconds for the Los Angeles Clippers in what would be his only NBA appearance.

53. ONLY ONE PLAYER HAS EVER COMMITTED SEVEN FOULS IN AN NBA GAME.

Cal Bowdler accomplished the feat in 1999 when the referee lost track of the number of fouls he had committed. The scorekeeper only noticed the blunder after the game was over.

54. IN 2015, GUARD LUKE RIDNOUR WAS TRADED AN ASTONISHING FOUR TIMES IN SIX DAYS.

Ultimately, he chose to sit out the season and retired the next year.

55. HALL OF FAMER DENNIS RODMAN IS GENERALLY CONSIDERED TO BE ONE OF THE GREATEST DEFENSIVE PLAYERS IN NBA HISTORY—BUT HE ALMOST NEVER MADE IT TO THE LEAGUE.

After high school, he found work as an overnight janitor at Dallas Fort Worth International Airport, and he wasn't drafted into the NBA until the age of 25.

56. IN 1991, A NEW WOMEN'S BASKETBALL LEAGUE CALLED THE LIBERTY BASKETBALL ASSOCIATION PLAYED ITS FIRST GAME, WHICH WAS BROADCAST ON ESPN.

Unfortunately, it would also be its last game, as the league unceremoniously folded shortly thereafter.

57. THE HIGHEST-SCORING GAME IN NCAA BASKETBALL HISTORY WAS A 1992 GAME BETWEEN TROY STATE AND DEVRY INSTITUTE THAT ENDED IN AN ASTONISHING SCORE OF 258-141. (TROY STATE WAS THE VICTOR.)

58. THANKS TO EJECTIONS, FOULS, AND INJURIES, ALABAMA HAD TO PLAY THE FINAL TEN MINUTES OF A 2017 COLLEGE BASKETBALL GAME AGAINST MINNESOTA WITH JUST THREE PLAYERS.

Amazingly, they actually outscored Minnesota during that time, and very nearly won the game.

59. NANCY LIEBERMAN BECAME THE FIRST WOMAN TO PLAY FOR A MEN'S PROFESSIONAL BASKETBALL TEAM WHEN SHE SUITED UP FOR THE SPRINGFIELD FAME OF THE UNITED STATES BASKETBALL LEAGUE (USBL) IN 1986.

She later became the first woman to coach a men's professional basketball team when she became head coach of the Texas Legends in the NBA Developmental League.

60. HALL OF FAME CENTER TIM DUNCAN HAS A TATTOO OF MERLIN (YES, MERLIN THE WIZARD) ON HIS CHEST. HE WAS ALSO NICKNAMED "MR. SPOCK" DURING COLLEGE AND IS KNOWN TO BE AN AVID DUNGEONS & DRAGONS PLAYER.

61. TRUE OR FALSE: MORE #1 PICKS IN THE MODERN NBA DRAFT HAVE BEEN BORN IN NEW YORK CITY THAN ANY OTHER CITY.

FALSE. Incredibly, Melbourne, Australia, has produced the most #1 picks (Ben Simmons, Kyrie Irving, and Andrew Bogut).

62. TRUE OR FALSE: LEGENDARY GUARD JOHN STOCKTON NEVER RECORDED A REGULAR-SEASON TRIPLE-DOUBLE.

TRUE. Despite being the all-time leader in both assists and steals (both by a wide margin), John Stockton never registered a regular-season triple-double in his entire career (though he did ultimately record one in the playoffs).

63. TRUE OR FALSE: ONLY ONE UNDRAFTED PLAYER HAS EVER MADE IT TO THE NBA HALL OF FAME.

TRUE. As of 2023, Ben Wallace remains the only undrafted player to be inducted into the Hall of Fame.

64. TRUE OR FALSE: MORE OFTEN THAN NOT, ALL FOUR #1 SEEDS MAKE THE FINAL FOUR OF THE NCAA MEN'S BASKETBALL TOURNAMENT.

FALSE. As of 2023, the top seeds have all made the Final Four together just once. In 2008, Kansas, Memphis, North Carolina, and UCLA all made it.

65. TRUE OR FALSE: SINCE 1993, MORE CANADIAN TEAMS HAVE WON THE NBA CHAMPIONSHIP THAN THE STANLEY CUP.

TRUE. It's a bit embarrassing for a country known for its hockey dominance, but no Canadian team has won the Stanley Cup since the Montreal Canadiens in 1993. The Toronto Raptors, on the other hand, won the NBA Championship in 2019.

66. TRUE OR FALSE: LARRY O'BRIEN, THE MAN FOR WHOM THE NBA CHAMPIONSHIP TROPHY IS NAMED, WAS PRESENT AT THE JFK ASSASSINATION.

TRUE. Yes, O'Brien was in the presidential motorcade the day President Kennedy was killed.

• 67 •

TRUE OR FALSE: NO MEN WERE ALLOWED TO WATCH THE VERY FIRST WOMEN'S BASKETBALL GAME.

TRUE. The first women's basketball team was organized in 1892 at Smith College in Northampton, Massachusetts. Just one year later, the team played its first game... and no men were allowed to watch.

68. TRUE OR FALSE: NBA JOURNEYMAN LANCE STEPHENSON JR.'S FULL FIRST NAME IS ACTUALLY "LANCELOT."

FALSE. No, but the Stephenson family does have an interesting relationship with names. Lance has a little brother...and his name is "Lantz."

69. TRUE OR FALSE: CHARLES BARKLEY USED TO PLAY NBA GAMES WITH HIS BELLY BUTTON STUFFED FULL OF VASELINE.

TRUE. This is, somehow, true. Barkley used to get terribly chapped lips and used Vaseline for relief during games.

70. TRUE OR FALSE: NBA LEGEND A. C. GREEN HAD CHRONIC HICCUPS THAT ONLY ABATED WHEN HE WAS EXERTING HIMSELF. AS A RESULT, HE ONLY EVER GOT TWO HOURS OF SLEEP AT NIGHT.

FALSE. For some reason, this has become a popular urban legend, but basketball historians generally agree it is not true.

71. TRUE OR FALSE: PAUL GEORGE'S NAME IS A BIT OF A FAMILY TRADITION—HIS PARENTS ARE NAMED PAUL AND PAULETTE.

TRUE. Believe it or not, it's true. Paulette may not be the most common name, but credit to the family for leaning into the interesting coincidence.

72. TRUE OR FALSE: COMBINED, THE CELTICS AND LAKERS HAVE WON MORE THAN HALF OF ALL NBA CHAMPIONSHIPS.

FALSE. But it's close. As of 2023, each team has 17 championships, combining for 34 of the 77 total championships in NBA history.

73. TRUE OR FALSE: NO PLAYER IN NBA HISTORY HAS WORN THE NUMBER 69.

TRUE. The number seems to be unofficially banned—the NBA reportedly denied Dennis Rodman's request to wear 69 when he signed with the Dallas Mavericks.

74. TRUE OR FALSE: WHILE UMBC DEFEATED VIRGINIA IN 2018 TO BECOME THE FIRST #16 SEED TO DEFEAT A #1 SEED IN THE NCAA MEN'S BASKETBALL TOURNAMENT, NO #16 SEED HAS EVER WON IN THE WOMEN'S TOURNAMENT.

FALSE. In fact, the feat had already long since been accomplished in the women's tournament. In 1998, Harvard defeated top-seeded Stanford, 20 years before UMBC's historic upset!

• 75 •

TRUE OR FALSE: NO WOMAN HAS EVER FILLED THE ROLE OF HEAD COACH IN THE NBA.

FALSE: In 2020, Spurs assistant coach Becky Hammon became the first woman to act as an NBA head coach when Spurs head coach Gregg Popovich was ejected from a game.

[Hockey]

No one has ever dominated a sport the way Wayne Gretzky dominated hockey, and it won't shock you to learn that "The Great One" features heavily in this section. But Gretzky was far from the only NHL star to make waves during his career. NHL fans have seen a kindergarten teacher go on to become a Hall of Famer and a player traded for $1 win four Stanley Cups. They've watched a fraudster purchase an NHL franchise, and another franchise draft a fictional player. It's a unique game that seems to grow more popular with each passing year—and with stories like those, it's not hard to see why.

1. **THERE ARE NUMEROUS MISTAKES AND MISSPELLINGS ON THE STANLEY CUP, INCLUDING THE 1971–72 BRUINS BEING LISTED AS THE "BQSTQN BRUINS."**

2. **THE NEW YORK RANGERS GOT THEIR NAME BASED ON A PUN.**

   The team owner at the time was nicknamed "Tex," and when the team was founded they were immediately dubbed "Tex's Rangers."

3. **AS OF THIS WRITING, 17 WOMEN HAVE HAD THEIR NAMES ENGRAVED ON THE STANLEY CUP.**

4. **ALBERTINE LAPENSÉE WAS A HOCKEY SUPERSTAR FROM THE TIME SHE WAS 16 YEARS OLD. FROM 1915 TO 1918, THE CORNWALL VICTORIAS ARE BELIEVED TO HAVE NEVER LOST A GAME WHEN SHE WAS IN THE LINEUP.**

   She once scored 15 goals in a single game, but elected to hang up her skates before the age of 20 when the team refused to fairly compensate her.

5. **ANGELA JAMES, OFTEN KNOWN AS THE "WAYNE GRETZKY OF WOMEN'S HOCKEY," WAS ONE OF HOCKEY'S FIRST TRUE FEMALE SUPERSTARS.**

   Following her 20-year career, she was inducted into the Hockey Hall of Fame, the International Ice Hockey Federation Hall of Fame, and the Canada Sports Hall of Fame. She is among the first women, Black women, and openly gay women in the Hockey Hall of Fame.

6. **WAYNE GRETZKY WOULD STILL BE THE NHL'S ALL-TIME POINTS LEADER EVEN IF HE HAD NEVER SCORED A SINGLE GOAL. (IN HOCKEY, BOTH GOALS AND ASSISTS ARE CONSIDERED "POINTS.")**

7. **ON A SIMILAR NOTE, EVEN IF WAYNE GRETZKY HAD NEVER SCORED A GOAL, HE WOULD STILL HAVE RECORDED 11 STRAIGHT 100-POINT SEASONS AND WON FOUR SCORING TITLES.**
The man was truly incredible.

8. **MARGUERITE NORRIS BECAME TEAM PRESIDENT OF THE DETROIT RED WINGS IN 1952, MAKING HER THE FIRST WOMAN TO HOLD SUCH A POSITION.**
Her reign was brief, but in her three seasons at the top, the Red Wings won the Stanley Cup twice. Norris is the first woman to have her name on the Stanley Cup trophy.

9. **THE FLORIDA PANTHERS REPEATEDLY TRIED TO EXPLOIT A DRAFT LOOPHOLE INVOLVING LEAP YEARS TO DRAFT ALEX OVECHKIN BEFORE HE WAS OFFICIALLY ELIGIBLE FOR THE NHL DRAFT. (IT DID NOT WORK.)**

10. **IN 1974, THE BUFFALO SABRES GENERAL MANAGER WAS FRUSTRATED BY HOW LONG IT TOOK TO CONDUCT THE NHL DRAFT. SO FRUSTRATED, IN FACT, THAT HE CONSPIRED TO INVENT AND DRAFT A FICITIONAL JAPANESE PLAYER NAMED "TARO TSUJIMOTO" TO MAKE A MOCKERY OF THE PROCEEDINGS.**
The team didn't admit the ruse until training camp.

• 11 •

THE BUFFALO SABRES ONCE LOST A GAME IN OVERTIME WHEN THE PUCK BECAME LODGED IN GOALIE MIKE SMITH'S PANTS AND HE DRIFTED BACKWARDS INTO THE GOAL. THE "BUTT GOAL" BECAME LEGENDARY.

• 12 •

THE TORONTO MAPLE
LEAFS ONCE LOST A
GAME TO THE CAROLINA
HURRICANES DESPITE
THE FACT THAT THE
HURRICANES WERE FORCED
TO PUT A 42-YEAR-OLD
ZAMBONI DRIVER IN NET
WHEN BOTH OF THEIR
GOALIES WENT DOWN
WITH INJURIES.

13. FROM 1981 TO 2001, THERE WERE ONLY THREE WINNERS OF THE ART ROSS TROPHY FOR NHL SCORING LEADER (WAYNE GRETZKY, MARIO LEMIUEX, AND JAROMIR JAGR).

14. IN 2018, BRUINS FORWARD BRAD MARCHAND WAS OFFICIALLY WARNED BY THE NHL TO STOP LICKING OPPOSING PLAYERS OR HE WOULD BE SUSPENDED.

15. THE FASTEST HAT TRICK IN NHL HISTORY WAS SCORED BY CHICAGO BLACKHAWKS PLAYER BILL MOSIENKO IN JUST 21 SECONDS.

16. FORWARD PASSES WERE NOT ALLOWED IN THE NHL UNTIL 1929.

17. MAPLE LEAFS FORWARD DARRYL SITTLER IS THE ONLY PLAYER IN NHL HISTORY TO SCORE DOUBLE-DIGIT POINTS IN AN NHL GAME.
During that game, he also became the most recent player to score six goals in a game.

18. NHL PUCKS ARE KEPT FROZEN IN AN ICEBOX UNTIL THEY ARE NEEDED.

19. HOCKEY ONLY BECAME CANADA'S OFFICIAL WINTER SPORT IN 1994.

Until that time, lacrosse was the country's only official sport (today, lacrosse is Canada's official summer sport).

20. MAPLE LEAFS WINGER KEN DORATY IS THE ONLY PLAYER IN NHL HISTORY TO SCORE A HAT TRICK IN OVERTIME.

The NHL has since switched to a sudden-death overtime format, so his record will probably stand forever.

21. A "GORDIE HOWE HAT TRICK" IS THE UNOFFICIAL TERM FOR WHEN A PLAYER RECORDS A GOAL, AN ASSIST, AND A FIGHT IN THE SAME GAME.

Despite its name, Gordie Howe himself only achieved the trifecta twice in his lengthy career.

22. GOALIE GLENN HALL PLAYED 502 CONSECUTIVE GAMES IN NET—AN NHL RECORD WIDELY CONSIDERED TO BE UNBREAKABLE.

Even so, Hall was most well-known for his pregame ritual: before each game he would vomit, then reportedly drink a glass of orange juice.

23. LONG BEFORE KRIS DRAPER BECAME A FOUR-TIME STANLEY CUP CHAMPION, THE WINNIPEG JETS TRADED HIM TO THE DETROIT RED WINGS FOR $1.

• 24 •

IN 1979, BOSTON BRUINS
PLAYER MIKE MILBURY
CLIMBED INTO THE
STANDS DURING A BRAWL
WITH THE NEW YORK
RANGERS AND BEAT
A RANGERS FAN WITH
HIS OWN SHOE.

• 25 •

IN 1992, MANON RHÉAUME BECAME THE FIRST WOMAN TO APPEAR IN AN NHL EXHIBITION GAME.

She played in several preseason games for the Tampa Bay Lighting across 1992 and 1993, and in doing so became the first woman to play professionally in any of the major North American sports.

26. HALL OF FAME BRUINS DEFENSEMAN RAY BOURQUE WOULD CHANGE THE LACES OF HIS SKATES BEFORE EVERY GAME—AND DURING EVERY INTERMISSION.

27. THE FIRST WOMAN TO SUIT UP FOR A MEN'S ICE HOCKEY TEAM WAS JENNY HANLEY, WHO PLAYED GOALIE FOR THE HAMLINE UNIVERSITY MEN'S HOCKEY TEAM IN 1991.

Not only did she play, she made 26 saves and led her team to victory!

28. LONGTIME VANCOUVER CANUCKS DEFENSEMAN KEVIN BIEKSA EARNED HIS FIRST NHL CONTRACT AFTER FIGHTING TEAMMATE FEDOR FEDOROV OUTSIDE A BAR AND KNOCKING HIM DOWN WITH ONE PUNCH.

The Canucks general manager was impressed!

29. THE FIRST OWNER OF THE TAMPA BAY LIGHTNING WAS A JAPANESE REAL ESTATE COMPANY RUN BY A MAN HEAVILY RUMORED TO BE A HIGH-RANKING MEMBER OF THE YAKUZA.

30. IN 1996, A MAN NAMED JOHN SPANO PURCHASED THE NEW YORK ISLANDERS FOR $165 MILLION. THE PROBLEM? SPANO WAS A HOAXER WHO HAD LIED ABOUT EVERYTHING FROM HIS ASSETS TO HIS HIGH SCHOOL EDUCATION.

It took almost a year, but he was ousted from ownership and later imprisoned for fraud.

31. **THE ORIGINAL TEAM COLORS FOR THE BOSTON BRUINS WERE BROWN AND GOLD BECAUSE THE TEAM OWNER WANTED THEM TO MATCH THE BRANDING OF THE GROCERY STORE CHAIN HE OWNED.**

32. **ST. LOUIS BLUES WINGER MIKE DANTON WAS ARRESTED IN 2004 FOR ATTEMPTING TO HIRE A HITMAN TO KILL HIS AGENT.**

He was imprisoned until 2009, but by 2011 was playing professional hockey again. He never made it back to the NHL, but played in leagues throughout Europe and Asia.

33. **DURING HIS SECOND SEASON, RANGERS FORWARD ALEX KOVALEV DEVELOPED A REPUTATION FOR STAYING ON THE ICE TOO LONG.**

To send him a message, Rangers coach Mike Keenan forced him to stay on the ice for more than seven straight minutes— something unheard of in the NHL. Unfortunately for Keenan, it didn't seem to occur to Kovalev that this was a punishment.

34. **THE ST. LOUIS BLUES ALMOST RELOCATED TO SASKATOON IN 1983.**

When the move was voted down by the NHL owners, the Blues sat out the NHL draft in protest. It remains the only time that has ever happened.

· 35 ·

FORMER WASHINGTON
CAPITALS GOALIE BRADEN
HOLTBY WAS ONCE
BARRED FROM ENTERING
CANADA WITH THE REST
OF HIS TEAM BECAUSE
HE LACKED THE PROPER
PAPERWORK FOR HIS
TWO PET TORTOISES.

• 36 •

THE WASHINGTON CAPITALS WON JUST EIGHT GAMES DURING THE 1975-76 SEASON, BUT THEY DID WIN THEIR FINAL GAME.

Afterward, the team celebrated in the locker room and passed around a trash can as if it were the Stanley Cup. They even did a lap of the arena with it.

37. IN 1998, BLUES DEFENSEMAN CHRIS PRONGER WAS STRUCK IN THE CHEST WITH A PUCK AND WENT INTO CARDIAC ARREST CAUSED BY COMMOTIO CORDIS, A RARE CONDITION WHERE AN IMPACT THAT OCCURS AT A CERTAIN POINT DURING THE HEARTBEAT CAN TEMPORARILY STOP THE HEART.

38. SINCE TIES WERE ELIMINATED IN THE NHL, THE LOSING TEAM IN AN OVERTIME GAME STILL RECEIVES ONE POINT (OFTEN DUBBED THE "LOSER POINT"), WHILE THE WINNER RECEIVES TWO POINTS.

But if a team pulls their goalie during the overtime period, they forfeit their right to the loser point.

39. STARS WINGER ALEXANDER RADULOV ONCE HAD TO WEAR A FAN'S REPLICA JERSEY DURING A PRESEASON GAME BECAUSE THE JERSEY THE TEAM PROVIDED FOR HIM DIDN'T FIT.

40. DURING THE 2011 STANLEY CUP FINALS, THE BRUINS AND CANUCKS WERE TIED THREE GAMES TO THREE, WITH EACH TEAM WINNING ALL OF THEIR HOME GAMES. BEFORE GAME 7 IN VANCOUVER, INJURED BRUINS WINGER NATHAN HORTON EMPTIED A WATER BOTTLE FILLED WITH MELTED ICE FROM THE BRUINS HOME ARENA ONTO THE PLAYING SURFACE.

The gambit worked: the Bruins won game 7 and took home the Stanley Cup.

41. WOMEN'S HOCKEY WAS SO POPULAR IN CANADA DURING THE 1930S THAT ONE TEAM, THE PRESTON RIVULETTES, WAS PLANNING A TOUR OF EUROPE TO SHOWCASE THEIR SKILLS UNTIL THE START OF WORLD WAR II DERAILED THEIR PLANS.

42. WITH 2,861, WAYNE GRETZKY AND HIS BROTHER BRENT HOLD THE RECORD FOR THE MOST COMBINED POINTS SCORED BY A PAIR OF BROTHERS IN THE NHL.

Wayne contributed 2,857 of those points. Brent contributed four. (Notably, the Sutter brothers have now combined for more points than the Gretzkys—but there are six of them!)

43. WHEN BARRY TABOBONDUNG WAS DRAFTED BY THE PHILADELPHIA FLYERS IN 1981, HE WAS SO EXCITED THAT HE TRIED TO CLIMB OVER A ROW OF SEATS TO GET TO THE STAGE.

Unfortunately, his foot became caught in the seat, and it took arena staff over two hours to free him by removing the entire row of seats.

44. THE FIRST WOMEN'S CLUB HOCKEY TEAM WAS FORMED AT QUEEN'S UNIVERSITY IN KINGSTON, ONTARIO.

The team took to calling themselves the "Love-Me-Littles" due to pushback and discrimination from the community.

45. WHEN LONGTIME SHARKS GOALIE EVGENI NABOKOV FIRST CAME TO THE US TO PLAY HOCKEY, HE TOLD HIS TEAMMATES TO CALL HIM "JOHN" BECAUSE HE DIDN'T THINK ANYONE WOULD BE ABLE TO PRONOUNCE HIS REAL NAME.

• 46 •

ANGELA RUGGIERO
BECAME THE FIRST
WOMAN TO APPEAR IN A
PROFESSIONAL HOCKEY
GAME AT A POSITION
OTHER THAN GOALIE WHEN
SHE SUITED UP FOR THE
TULSA OILERS IN 2005.

More amazingly, since her brother, Bill
Ruggiero, also played for the team, they became
the first ever brother-sister duo to play together!

THE CANADIAN WOMEN'S HOCKEY TEAM FAMOUSLY (AND CONTROVERSIALLY) WORE ALL-PINK UNIFORMS DURING THE 1990 WOMEN'S WORLD CHAMPIONSHIPS.

But the pink didn't stop there: during the event, the Zamboni driver wore a flamingo costume and decorated his ride with toy flamingos. Oh, brother.

48. BEFORE WAYNE GRETZKY'S FINAL GAME, THE LYRICS TO THE AMERICAN AND CANADIAN NATIONAL ANTHEMS WERE CHANGED TO INCLUDE CRINGEWORTHY LINES LIKE "O'ER THE LAND OF WAYNE GRETZKY," AND "WE'RE GONNA MISS YOU, WAYNE GRETZKY."

49. FORWARD NATHAN HORTON IS CREDITED WITH A GOAL IN A GAME HE DID NOT PLAY IN.

Horton scored during a game that had to be suspended due to a medical emergency, but did not play in the rescheduled game due to injury. The game started over, but Horton's goal stood, resulting in a stat line of one goal, zero minutes played.

50. THE DAY HE WAS DEALT FROM THE OILERS TO THE KINGS, WAYNE GRETZKY WAS HOUSESITTING FOR HIS FRIEND, ACTOR ALAN THICKE.

He was also babysitting Thicke's son, who would grow up to be famous recording artist Robin Thicke.

51. WOMEN'S HOCKEY DATES BACK AS FAR AS THE 1800S, WITH THE EARLIEST KNOWN REPORT OF A GAME OCCURRING IN FEBRUARY 1891.

While women's hockey is growing in popularity today, it is hardly a new phenomenon!

52. MONTREAL CANADIENS MASCOT "YOUPPI!" WAS ORIGINALLY THE MASCOT FOR A DIFFERENT MONTREAL TEAM: MLB'S MONTREAL EXPOS.

When the Expos relocated to Washington, DC, the Canadiens "adopted" the mascot as their own.

53. AT AGE NINE, ABBY HOFFMAN WANTED TO PLAY HOCKEY BADLY ENOUGH THAT IN 1956 SHE PRETENDED TO BE A BOY TO JOIN HER LOCAL LEAGUE.

She was dropped from the team when her birth certificate was revealed, but her family appealed the decision all the way up to the Ontario Supreme Court. Unfortunately, it did not go her way—but Hoffman would go on to become a women's hockey Olympic legend.

54. THE FLEDGLING CALIFORNIA GOLDEN SEALS ONCE PAID A WOMAN TO CIRCLE THE ARENA WEARING ONLY ICE SKATES, WITH "SEALS" PAINTED ACROSS HER BODY. THE GOAL WAS TO CREATE BUZZ FOR THE TEAM, AND, WELL, IT DIDN'T EXACTLY WORK.

55. TOM BARRASSO REMAINS THE ONLY GOALIE TO ENTER THE NHL DIRECTLY FROM HIGH SCHOOL.

It worked out pretty well for him: he won the Vezina Trophy as the league's top goaltender in his very first season and would go on to win two Stanley Cups and be inducted into the NHL Hall of Fame.

56. GAME 2 OF THE 1951 STANLEY CUP SEMIFINALS BETWEEN THE BOSTON BRUINS AND THE TORONTO MAPLE LEAFS ENDED IN A 1-1 TIE.

How can a playoff game end in a tie? Well, the game was played on Saturday, and Toronto had an ordinance that made it illegal to play on Sunday. When the game went to overtime and the clock approached midnight, it was declared a tie.

57. THE NATIONAL WOMEN'S HOCKEY LEAGUE (NWHL) MAY NOT HAVE LASTED LONG, BUT IT INCLUDED SOME MEMORABLE TEAM NAMES.

Among the teams to play during the league's eight-year run were the Calgary Oval X-Treme, the Montreal Jofa Titan, and the Saskatchewan Prairie Ice.

58. CALGARY FLAMES GOALIE JAMIE MCLENNAN WAS GIVEN A FIVE-GAME SUSPENSION FOR SLASHING RED WINGS FORWARD JOHAN FRANZÉN DURING A PLAY-OFF GAME. HOWEVER, MCLENNAN NEVER PLAYED ANOTHER GAME IN THE NHL—WHICH MEANS HE NEVER SERVED THE SUSPENSION, AND TECHNICALLY REMAINS SUSPENDED LONG INTO RETIREMENT.

59. MARIO LEMIEUX ONCE SCORED FIVE GOALS IN FIVE DIFFERENT WAYS DURING AN NHL GAME: HE SCORED AN EVEN-STRENGTH GOAL, A POWER-PLAY GOAL, A SHORTHANDED GOAL, A PENALTY SHOT GOAL, AND AN EMPTY NET GOAL.

He is the only player to ever accomplish this feat (though, to be fair, scoring five goals in a game at all is pretty rare).

60. WAYNE GRETZKY WAS THE FASTEST PLAYER TO SCORE 1,000 POINTS.

He was also the second fastest: Gretzky went from 1,000 points to 2,000 points faster than any other player went from 0 to 1,000.

61. TRUE OR FALSE: NO PLAYER IN NHL HISTORY HAS EVER SCORED A SHORTHANDED HAT TRICK.

FALSE. During the 1990–91 season, Calgary Flames forward Theo Fleury scored three shorthanded goals against the St. Louis Blues. He remains the only player to accomplish the feat.

62. TRUE OR FALSE: CANADIAN CAPTAIN MARIE-PHILIP POULIN SCORED THE GAME-WINNING GOAL IN NOT ONE, NOT TWO, BUT THREE GOLD MEDAL GAMES DURING HER OLYMPIC CAREER.

TRUE. Canada's "Captain Clutch" won gold for Canada in 2010, 2014, and 2022.

63. TRUE OR FALSE: WAYNE GRETZKY ENTERED THE NHL AS THE FIRST OVERALL DRAFT PICK.

FALSE. In fact, Gretzky was never drafted at all: he signed on to play in the World Hockey Association and entered the NHL when his contract was later sold to Edmonton.

64. TRUE OR FALSE: THE NHL WAS FORMED SPECIFICALLY TO GET RID OF ONE BAD OWNER.

TRUE. The National Hockey Association was disbanded, and all of its teams reconstituted as the National Hockey League... except for the Toronto Blueshirts and their unpopular owner, Eddie Livingstone.

65. TRUE OR FALSE: THE LOS ANGELES KINGS DRAFTED TWO NHL HALL OF FAMERS IN 1984.

FALSE. They drafted one hockey Hall of Famer (Luc Robitaille) and one baseball Hall of Famer (Tom Glavine). It's particularly funny that Glavine was selected before Robitaille!

• 66 •

TRUE OR FALSE: IN 2024, A WOMEN'S HOCKEY LEAGUE WAS FOUNDED WITH AN INTERESTING TWIST: NO TEAM NAMES OR LOGOS.

TRUE. In 2024, the Professional Women's Hockey League (PWHL) began play with six teams, none of which had a name or logo. The league chose instead to foreground the talent of the individual players.

67. TRUE OR FALSE: NO GOALIE HAS EVER SCORED AN NHL GOAL.

FALSE. But it is very, very rare. Only 14 goalies have ever scored an NHL goal, and just two have scored more than one. Martin Brodeur is the only goalie to score three goals, with two regular-season goals and one playoff goal on his résumé.

68. TRUE OR FALSE: THE FIRST NHL TEAMS WERE THE BRUINS, BLACKHAWKS, RED WINGS, CANADIENS, RANGERS, AND MAPLE LEAFS.

FALSE. While those teams are considered to be the NHL's "Original Six," the first NHL season actually featured just four teams: the Montreal Wanderers, Montreal Canadiens, Toronto Arenas, and Ottawa Senators. Unfortunately, the Wanderers never finished that first season: the team folded after its arena burned down.

69. TRUE OR FALSE: THE MAPLE LEAFS ARE CALLED THE "LEAFS" RATHER THAN THE "LEAVES" BECAUSE OF A GRAMMATICAL ERROR EARLY IN THE TEAM'S HISTORY THAT NO ONE CORRECTED.

FALSE. Actually, the Maple Leafs are not named after actual maple leaves, but after the Maple Leaf armbands worn by Canadian soldiers in World War I.

70. TRUE OR FALSE: UNTIL THE 1940S, GOALIES USED TO SERVE THEIR OWN PENALTIES, FORCING A POSITION PLAYER TO TEMPORARILY COVER THE NET.

TRUE. Until the 1941–42 season, if a goalie committed a penalty, he went to the box. As you can imagine, this made a penalty on a goalie particularly devastating.

71. **TRUE OR FALSE: THE US AND CANADA WERE ONCE SO DOMINANT AT WOMEN'S HOCKEY THAT THE OLYMPICS THREATENED TO REMOVE THE SPORT FROM COMPETITION.**

TRUE. The US and Canada were so dominant during the 2010 Olympics that the International Olympic Committee threatened to put an end to the event due to lack of competition. The International Ice Hockey Federation then invested more than $2 million in female hockey programs around the world to help other countries catch up.

72. **TRUE OR FALSE: THE PITTSBURGH PENGUINS' FIRST MASCOT WAS AN ACTUAL PENGUIN WITH CUSTOM-MADE SKATES.**

TRUE. Unfortunately, the team wasn't well equipped to care for a penguin, and "Penguin Pete" died of pneumonia after his nesting area was kept too warm.

73. **TRUE OR FALSE: ICING WAS ORIGINALLY A TWO-MINUTE PENALTY.**

FALSE. Actually, icing wasn't penalized at all until the late 1930s, after the Bruins iced the puck 87 times in a single game to make a point about how frustrating the practice was to watch.

74. **TRUE OR FALSE: FRANK J. SELKE'S NAME APPEARS ON THE STANLEY CUP WITH THE UNFORTUNATE PARENTHETICAL "ASS MAN."**

TRUE. Selke was the assistant general manager for the Maple Leafs in 1945, and apparently no one thought about how unfortunate that abbreviation was.

TRUE OR FALSE: HALL OF FAME WINGER TEEMU SELÄNNE SPENT THREE YEARS WORKING AS A KINDERGARTEN TEACHER IN FINLAND BEFORE FINALLY GETTING A SHOT TO PLAY PROFESSIONAL HOCKEY.

TRUE: He's a legend now, but at the time it was unclear whether he would ever get a shot to play pro hockey.

[Soccer]

Let's first address the elephant in the room. This book is written by an American, which means "the beautiful game" will be referred to as soccer. If that offends your sensibilities, just flip ahead a few pages: you'll find that "soccer" was originally coined not by the Americans, but by the British! Soccer remains one of the most popular sports in the world for a reason. It's simple to learn, but difficult to master, and those who do become legends the world over. Stars like Pelé and Maradona remain household names decades after their careers ended, while clubs like Barcelona, Arsenal, and Bayern Munich have fans in every country on earth. But soccer doesn't just have stars: it has weirdos too. Like a player who can't stop biting and another who almost burned down his own house. Soccer may be the beautiful game…but it isn't always pretty.

1. THE WORLD CUP HAS NEVER BEEN WON BY A TEAM WHOSE MANAGER DID NOT COME FROM THE TEAM'S COUNTRY.

2. WHILE PLAYERS LIKE PELÉ, RONALDO, OR NEYMAR ARE MORE WELL-KNOWN, BRAZIL'S ALL-TIME LEADING GOAL SCORER IS ACTUALLY MARTA VIEIRA DA SILVA (MONONYMOUSLY KNOWN AS MARTA).
She scored 115 goals for the Brazil women's national football team before retiring from international play in 2023—far more than Neymar, who leads the men with 79 goals (as of this publication).

3. LEICESTER CITY WON THE ENGLISH PREMIER LEAGUE IN 2016, DESPITE OPENING THE SEASON WITH JUST 5,000 TO 1 ODDS.
By betting odds, it was the single biggest upset in the history of team sports.

4. THE MOST LOPSIDED VICTORY IN AN INTERNATIONAL SOCCER MATCH OCCURRED IN 2001, WHEN AUSTRALIA DOMINATED AMERICAN SAMOA AN ASTONISHING 31-0.

5. THE YOUNGEST PLAYER TO WIN THE WORLD CUP WAS BRAZILIAN LEGEND PELÉ, WHO WAS JUST 17 YEARS OLD WHEN BRAZIL WON THE TOURNAMENT IN 1958.
In 1994, Brazil won again...this time with 17-year-old Ronaldo on the team (Pelé was younger by a few days, however).

6. **IN 1992, DENMARK FAILED TO QUALIFY FOR THE EUROPEAN CHAMPIONSHIP TOURNAMENT...BUT MANAGED TO WIN IT ANYWAY.**
They were granted a last-minute entry after FIFA placed a ban on Yugoslavia.

7. **IN 1921, WOMEN'S SOCCER WAS INCREDIBLY POPULAR IN ENGLAND—BUT THE FA (THE SPORT'S GOVERNING BODY IN ENGLAND) INSTITUTED A BAN ON WOMEN'S SOCCER THAT WOULD ULTIMATELY LAST 51 YEARS.**
The absurd justification? The FA "felt impelled to express the strong opinion that the game of football is quite unsuitable for females and should not be encouraged."

8. **BRAZILIAN GOALKEEPER ROGÉRIO CENI HAS ALMOST TWICE AS MANY GOALS AS ANY OTHER KEEPER, WITH 131 OVER THE COURSE OF HIS CAREER.**
Ceni was known for taking both free kicks and penalty kicks for his teams.

9. **DURING THE 1993–94 SEASON, AC MILAN FINISHED FIRST IN SERIE A, DESPITE SCORING JUST 36 GOALS IN 34 GAMES. (OF COURSE, IT HELPS THAT THEY ONLY CONCEDED 15.)**

10. **SPAIN WON THE 2010 WORLD CUP DESPITE SCORING JUST EIGHT GOALS DURING THE ENTIRE TOURNAMENT.**

• 11 •

WHEN STEFAN SCHWARZ TRANSFERRED TO SUNDERLAND, HIS NEW CONTRACT INCLUDED A "SPACE CLAUSE" THAT STATED HIS DEAL WOULD BECOME INVALID IF HE TRAVELED TO OUTER SPACE.

This wasn't as crazy as it sounds: Schwarz had expressed interest in space tourism, and the team did not want him engaging in such risky behavior.

• 12 •

IN 1920, ENGLAND'S DICK, KERR LADIES BECAME THE FIRST WOMEN'S TEAM TO PLAY A NIGHT MATCH AFTER THE TEAM RECEIVED PERMISSION FROM WINSTON CHURCHILL TO ILLUMINATE THE PITCH WITH TWO ANTIAIRCRAFT SEARCHLIGHTS.

13. WHILE THE US MEN'S NATIONAL TEAM OFTEN STRUGGLES TO QUALIFY FOR THE WORLD CUP, THE US WOMEN'S NATIONAL TEAM HAS WON THE TOURNAMENT FOUR TIMES—MORE THAN ANY OTHER COUNTRY!

14. THE 1980 COPA DEL REY FINAL WAS PLAYED BETWEEN REAL MADRID...AND REAL MADRID'S OWN RESERVE TEAM.

Unsurprisingly, Real Madrid won handily, defeating the reserves 6–1.

15. THE OLDEST INDEPENDENT SOCCER CLUB STILL IN EXISTENCE ISN'T A TEAM LIKE MANCHESTER UNITED OR BARCELONA—IT'S ENGLAND'S SHEFFIELD FC, WHICH WAS FOUNDED IN 1857.

16. IN 1991, THE FIRST WOMEN'S WORLD CUP WAS HELD...EXCEPT THAT'S NOT WHAT IT WAS CALLED.

FIFA wasn't quite ready to grant the new tournament the "World Cup" label, so the first event was known as the "1st FIFA World Championship for Women's Football for the M&M's Cup." Catchy, right?

17. JUST HOW POPULAR WAS WOMEN'S SOCCER IN ENGLAND? IN 1920, A CHARITY MATCH BETWEEN WOMEN'S TEAMS SET AN ATTENDANCE RECORD THAT WOULD NOT BE TOPPED UNTIL 2012!

Even factoring in the lengthy ban on women's soccer, that's an impressive feat.

18. THE 1958 WORLD CUP MARKS THE FIRST AND ONLY TIME THAT THE FOUR "HOME NATIONS" OF THE UNITED KINGDOM (ENGLAND, SCOTLAND, WALES, AND NORTHERN IRELAND) QUALIFIED FOR THE SAME WORLD CUP TOURNAMENT.

19. SOME 51 TEAMS HAVE COMPETED IN THE ENGLISH PREMIER LEAGUE SINCE IT WAS FOUNDED IN 1992. JUST SIX HAVE NEVER BEEN RELEGATED: ARSENAL, CHELSEA, EVERTON, LIVERPOOL, MANCHESTER UNITED, AND TOTTENHAM HOTSPUR.

20. IN 2007–08, DERBY COUNTY ENDED THE SEASON WITH JUST 11 POINTS, SETTING THE RECORD FOR THE FEWEST POINTS IN A PREMIER LEAGUE SEASON.
They won just one match all season, at one point going 32 consecutive matches without a victory.

21. SOCCER PITCHES ARE NOT UNIFORM IN SIZE.
Like baseball fields, they must conform to a certain range of dimensions, but that range can vary greatly.

22. BELIEVE IT OR NOT, THE TERM "SOCCER" ORIGINATED IN GREAT BRITAIN!

The formal name of the sport is "association football." British students took the "soc" from association and nicknamed it "soccer" in jest, but it caught on with Americans, who have stuck with the name ever since.

· 23 ·

THE ALL-TIME LEADER FOR INTERNATIONAL GOALS SCORED IS NOT PELÉ, MARADONA, OR MESSI: IT'S CANADIAN FORWARD CHRISTINE SINCLAIR.

Sinclair has scored 190 goals during her international career, easily topping the 128 scored by men's leader Cristiano Ronaldo. Amazingly, Sinclair and Ronaldo are still active as of this publication, and could both add to their totals.

· 24 ·

IN 1954, WORLD CUP FAVORITE SPAIN WAS ELIMINATED FROM TOURNAMENT QUALIFICATION IN A VERY STRANGE WAY: ITS TIEBREAKER WITH TURKEY WAS SETTLED BY THE DRAWING OF LOTS.

An Italian teenager was blindfolded and ultimately chose Turkey to move on to the knockout stage.

25. SHEFFIELD UNITED PLAYER KEITH GILLESPIE HOLDS THE DUBIOUS RECORD FOR THE FASTEST RED CARD IN A PREMIER LEAGUE MATCH.

Gillespie swung an elbow at his opponent just 12 seconds after coming on as a substitute and was promptly sent off. (Some argue that he was actually sent off after zero seconds, as he was technically sent off before play even resumed.)

26. DURING THE BAN ON WOMEN'S SOCCER IN ENGLAND, DICK, KERR LADIES TOURED THE US, WHERE THEY PLAYED A SERIES OF MATCHES AGAINST MEN'S TEAMS.

Of the nine matches played, Dick, Kerr Ladies won three, lost three, and tied three!

27. THIERRY HENRY'S HANDBALL WASN'T THE MOST IMPACTFUL IN WORLD CUP HISTORY. DURING A 1986 WORLD CUP QUARTERFINAL MATCH AGAINST ENGLAND, ARGENTINA LEGEND DIEGO MARADONA DEFLECTED THE BALL OVER ENGLAND'S KEEPER AND INTO THE NET USING HIS HAND.

The referees did not notice, and the incident became known as the "Hand of God" goal.

28. ENGLISH PREMIER LEAGUE CLUB ARSENAL WAS ORIGINALLY CALLED "WOOLRICH ARSENAL," AND LATER "THE ARSENAL."

In 1919, the name was shortened to just "Arsenal," allegedly to ensure the team would always be alphabetically near the top of the league.

29. MAJOR LEAGUE SOCCER (MLS), THE UNITED STATES'S PROFESSIONAL SOCCER LEAGUE, WAS CREATED NOT OUT OF PUBLIC DEMAND, BUT IN AN EFFORT TO BOLSTER THE US'S (SUCCESSFUL) BID FOR THE 1994 WORLD CUP.

30. WHILE SPORTS LIKE BASEBALL AND AMERICAN FOOTBALL REMAINED SEGREGATED WELL INTO THE 1900S, THE FIRST BLACK PROFESSIONAL SOCCER PLAYER WAS ARTHUR WHARTON, WHO PLAYED FOR ENGLAND'S ROTTERDAM UNITED IN 1889.

31. THE LARGEST SOCCER STADIUM IN THE WORLD ISN'T LOCATED IN ENGLAND OR BRAZIL—IT'S IN NORTH KOREA.

The Rungrado 1st of May Stadium is located in Pyongyang and can hold as many as 114,000 fans. (Some estimates say it can hold as many as 150,000.)

32. THE FASTEST GOAL IN THE HISTORY OF ASSOCIATION FOOTBALL TOOK PLACE DURING A WEST OF SCOTLAND SUPER LEAGUE FIRST DIVISION MATCH IN 2017, WHEN MARYHILL PLAYER GAVIN STOKES SCORED JUST 2.1 SECONDS INTO A MATCH AGAINST CLYDEBANK.

33. THE HIGHEST SCORING SOCCER MATCH OF ALL TIME WAS BETWEEN MADAGASCAN SIDES—AS ADEMA AND STADE OLYMPIQUE DE L'EMYRNE.

Adema won 149–0, in a match that saw l'Emyrne players angry about a prior refereeing decision score own goal after own goal in protest.

• 34 •

IN 1998, ENGLISH REFEREE MELVIN SYLVESTER AWARDED A RED CARD TO... HIMSELF.

While technically not allowed, he recused himself from the match after punching a player during an altercation.

• 35 •

WHEN A MALE
GOALKEEPER TOLD
SOCCER LEGEND LILY
PARR THAT NO WOMAN
COULD SCORE AGAINST
A MAN, SHE TOOK
UP THE CHALLENGE
AND ATTEMPTED A
PENALTY KICK.

Not only did she score, she reportedly broke
the goalie's wrist in the process.

36. ROUGHLY 70% OF ALL SOCCER BALLS ARE PRODUCED IN THE CITY OF SIALKOT IN NORTHEAST PAKISTAN.

37. IN 1966, THE ORIGINAL WORLD CUP TROPHY WAS STOLEN. FORTUNATELY, IT WAS FOUND JUST A WEEK LATER, THANKS TO THE VALIANT EFFORTS OF A SEARCH DOG NAMED PICKLES.

38. WHEN INTER MILAN SIGNED BRAZILIAN SUPERSTAR RONALDO IN 1997, THE CLUB TOOK THE #9 AWAY FROM IVÁN ZAMORANO AND AWARDED IT TO RONALDO.
Undeterred, Zamorano wore the number 18 for three years... but added a small plus sign between the 1 and the 8.

39. THE MUSIC VIDEO FOR JENNIFER LOPEZ'S "LET'S GET LOUD" WAS RECORDED DURING HER PERFORMANCE AT THE CLOSING CEREMONIES OF THE 1999 WOMEN'S WORLD CUP.

40. THE BALLON D'OR, CONSIDERED SOCCER'S TOP INDIVIDUAL AWARD, HAS BEEN AWARDED SINCE 1956. IT HAS ONLY BEEN AWARDED TO A GOALIE ONCE: LEV YASHIN IN 1963.

41. THE ONLY INTERNATIONAL TEAM IN THE WORLD THAT HAS PLAYED BRAZIL WITHOUT EVER LOSING IS NORWAY.
The nations have played four times, with Norway winning two and drawing two.

42. STRIKER DIDIER DROGBA PLAYED A CRUCIAL ROLE IN HELPING HIS NATIVE IVORY COAST PUT A STOP TO A CIVIL WAR.

After scoring a crucial goal to send the Ivory Coast to the World Cup for the first time, Drogba used his platform to urge the two warring factions to lay down their arms. Thanks to the global attention his plea received, peace negotiations resumed.

43. FAMED STRIKER GEORGE WEAH WON THE BALLON D'OR IN 1995...AND WAS ELECTED PRESIDENT OF LIBERIA IN 2018.

Weah remains the only African player to ever win the Ballon d'Or.

44. BRIANA SCURRY HAD A CAREER OF FIRSTS: NOT ONLY WAS SHE THE FIRST BLACK PLAYER ON THE US WOMEN'S NATIONAL SOCCER TEAM, SHE WAS ALSO THE FIRST OPENLY GAY PLAYER ON THE TEAM.

45. A 2005 STUDY FOUND THAT ROUGHLY 6% OF SOCCER INJURIES OCCUR NOT DURING PLAY, BUT WHILE CELEBRATING A GOAL.

46. THE RECORD FOR GOALS SCORED BY A PLAYER IN A SINGLE MATCH IS 16.

The feat was first accomplished by Racing Club de Lens player Stephan Stanis in 1942 and later equaled by Olympos Xylofagou player Panagiotis Pontikos in 2007.

· 47 ·

A DUTCH SOCCER CLUB ONCE SIGNED A CONTRACT WITH AN 18-MONTH-OLD BABY.

· 48 ·

IN THE 1950S, LEGENDARY ACTOR SEAN CONNERY WAS TALENTED ENOUGH ON THE PITCH THAT ENGLAND'S MANCHESTER UNITED OFFERED HIM A CONTRACT.

Fortunately for James Bond fans,
he turned it down.

49. THE GLAZER FAMILY WAS ONLY ABLE TO PURCHASE MANCHESTER UNITED AFTER A FEUD OVER A RACE-HORSE CRIPPLED RELATIONS BETWEEN THE TEAM'S OWNERSHIP AND THEN-MANAGER SIR ALEX FERGUSON.

50. STRIKER AND NOTORIOUS BAD BOY MARIO BALOTELLI NEARLY BURNED DOWN HIS OWN MANSION IN 2011 WHEN HE SET OFF DOZENS OF FIREWORKS IN A FIRST-FLOOR BATHROOM DURING A PARTY.

51. CELEBRITY CHEF AND *HELL'S KITCHEN* STAR GORDON RAMSAY WAS HEAVILY SCOUTED BY PROFESSIONAL SOCCER TEAMS, BUT HIS BURGEONING CAREER CAME TO AN END WHEN HE SUFFERED A MAJOR KNEE INJURY.

Seems like it all worked out for the best, though.

52. IN 2019, JAMAICA QUALIFIED FOR THE WOMEN'S WORLD CUP FOR THE FIRST TIME.

They have an unusual person to thank: Cedella Marley, eldest daughter of Bob Marley, played a key role in reviving the team after it was initially disbanded in 2008.

53. LEGENDARY GERMAN STRIKER ROBERT LEWANDOWSKI ONLY SLEEPS ON HIS LEFT SIDE.

He claims his doctor told him this would help preserve his right leg, which is his dominant shooting leg.

54. BRAZILIAN MIDFIELDER FORMIGA MAINTAINED A HIGH LEVEL OF PLAY ACROSS HER INCREDIBLE 26-YEAR INTERNATIONAL CAREER.

Formiga is the only player (man or woman) in history to appear in seven World Cups and seven Olympic Games.

55. TIRED OF PLAYING SECOND FIDDLE TO MEN, IN 1971 THE FEDERATION OF INDEPENDENT EUROPEAN FEMALE FOOTBALL (FIEFF) ORGANIZED AN UNOFFICIAL "WOMEN'S WORLD CUP."

The event took place in Mexico, where the men's World Cup had been held one year earlier, and drew massive crowds—including one game that brought in an estimated 110,000 spectators!

56. WHILE HIS RECORD HAS SINCE BEEN BROKEN, MANCHESTER UNITED DEFENDER AXEL TUANZEBE ONCE HELD THE GUINNESS WORLD RECORD FOR THE FASTEST GAME OF *HUNGRY HUNGRY HIPPOS*.

57. WHILE SERVING AS MANAGING DIRECTOR OF BIRMINGHAM CITY F.C., KARREN BRADY SOLD STRIKER PAUL PESCHISOLIDO TO STOKE CITY. WHY IS THAT NOTABLE?

Peschisolido was her future husband!

58. THE LONGEST NAME FOR A EUROPEAN PROFESSIONAL SOCCER CLUB BELONGS TO DUTCH SIDE "NOOIT OPGEVEN ALTIJD DOORZETTEN, AANGENAAM DOOR VERMAAK EN NUTTIG DOOR ONTSPANNING, COMBINATIE BREDA."

Unsurprisingly, the name is usually shortened to "NAC Breda."

59. MANCHESTER UNITED GOALIE ALEX STEPNEY ONCE YELLED AT HIS DEFENDERS SO HARD THAT HE DISLOCATED HIS OWN JAW. OUCH!

60. AS OF 2023, NO ENGLISH MANAGER HAS EVER WON THE ENGLISH PREMIER LEAGUE.

61. TRUE OR FALSE: A TEAM ONCE FINISHED AN ENTIRE SEASON WITHOUT LOSING A GAME BUT STILL FAILED TO WIN THE LEAGUE.

TRUE. In 1978–79, Perugia went an entire season undefeated but finished behind AC Milan in the Serie A standings.

62. TRUE OR FALSE: ECUADOR'S ANGIE PONCE ONCE SCORED AN ODD HAT TRICK: ONE GOAL AND TWO OWN GOALS.

TRUE. During the 2015 Women's World Cup, Ponce earned the dubious distinction of becoming the only woman in tournament history to score two own goals in one match. It wasn't all bad, though: in that same game, she also scored Ecuador's first goal in Women's World Cup history.

63. TRUE OR FALSE: PORTSMOUTH WON THE FA CUP A RECORD SIX TIMES IN A ROW.

FALSE. That said, Portsmouth did hold the trophy for a record seven years...but only because they won in 1939 and the tournament was not held again until after World War II.

64. TRUE OR FALSE: STOKE CITY ONCE PLAYED AN ENTIRE SEASON IN AMERICA.

TRUE. And they weren't alone! Stoke City, Wolverhampton, and Sunderland were all sent to the US to compete in the new United Soccer Association. Wolverhampton wound up winning the league, but it disbanded the following year and the teams returned to the UK.

65. TRUE OR FALSE: THE ATTENDANCE RECORD AT OLD TRAFFORD, MANCHESTER UNITED'S HOME STADIUM, WAS SET DURING A MANCHESTER UNITED VS. ARSENAL MATCH THAT DECIDED THAT YEAR'S PREMIER LEAGUE CHAMPION.

FALSE. In fact, the record was set during a game that didn't even involve Manchester United: it was set during a 1939 FA Cup semifinal match between Wolverhampton and Grimsby Town.

66. TRUE OR FALSE: LONGTIME CHELSEA MIDFIELDER JOHN OBI MIKEL WAS NAMED AFTER OBI-WAN KENOBI.

FALSE. No, but his name does have an interesting story: "Mikel" was an accidental misspelling of "Michael" by the Nigerian Football Association, but he liked it so much he decided to stick with it. Today, he is known as Mikel John Obi.

• 67 •

TRUE OR FALSE: THE WORLD'S OLDEST KNOWN SOCCER BALL BELONGED TO MARY QUEEN OF SCOTS.

TRUE. Mary Queen of Scots was purported to be a huge soccer fan, and the "World's Oldest Football" was discovered in the rafters of her former bedchamber in Stirling Castle. It is the oldest known soccer ball in existence and currently sits in the Stirling Smith Art Gallery and Museum.

68. **TRUE OR FALSE: LEGENDARY STRIKER CRISTIANO RONALDO WAS NAMED AFTER RONALD REAGAN.**

TRUE. This one is true. Reagan was president when Ronaldo was born, although his father gave him the name because Reagan was his favorite movie actor.

69. **TRUE OR FALSE: ENGLISH STRIKER GARY LINEKER ONCE POOPED HIS PANTS IN THE MIDDLE OF A WORLD CUP MATCH.**

TRUE. Lineker himself now laughs about it. He was struggling with a stomach illness the day of the match and lost control while making a tackle.

70. **TRUE OR FALSE: THE OLDEST PLAYER TO APPEAR IN A WORLD CUP MATCH WAS 51 YEARS OLD.**

FALSE. No, not quite that old. At 45 years, 161 days, Egypt's Essam El Hadary holds the record. In fact, only six other players over the age of 40 have ever appeared in a World Cup match!

71. **TRUE OR FALSE: AMERICAN HEAVYWEIGHT BOXER JOE LOUIS SIGNED TO PLAY FOR LIVERPOOL F.C. DURING WORLD WAR II.**

TRUE. Admittedly, it was more of a stunt than anything. But Louis did participate in a training session with the team.

72. TRUE OR FALSE: NO EUROPEAN PLAYER HAS EVER PLAYED TWO COMPETITIVE MATCHES IN A SINGLE DAY.

FALSE. Welsh legend Mark Hughes suited up for Wales to play a Euro qualifying match on November 11, 1987, then flew over to West Germany to play for Bayern Munich later that night.

73. TRUE OR FALSE: LIBYAN DICTATOR MUAMMAR GADDAFI ALMOST PURCHASED CRYSTAL PALACE.

TRUE. In 2004, the club was looking for buyers, and the chairman at the time made it clear he would consider an offer from Gaddafi if it was made.

74. TRUE OR FALSE: THE AUTHOR OF THIS BOOK ONCE APPEARED AS A US SUBSTITUTE DURING A WORLD CUP QUALIFYING MATCH.

FALSE. No. Absolutely not. Why would you think that?

· 75 ·

TRUE OR FALSE: CELERY IS EXPRESSLY BANNED AT CHELSEA'S STAMFORD BRIDGE STADIUM.

TRUE. Yes, the vegetable became associated with an unsavory chant favored by Chelsea fans, and it was thrown onto the pitch one too many times.

[The Olympics]

The Olympic Games represent the only time for certain sports to shine—be honest, have you ever watched "dressage" outside the context of the Olympics? From synchronized swimming and bobsledding to marathons and pole vaulting, the Olympic Games offer some of the world's greatest athletes the rare chance to showcase their skills on an international stage. Of course, the games also provide the opportunity to engage in some truly unique cheating. From pugilistic polo players to rewired épées, some impressively weird and wild things have happened on the Olympic stage!

1. **IN THE 1980S AND 90S, THE OLYMPICS FEATURED THE STRANGE SPORT OF SOLO SYNCHRONIZED SWIMMING.**
Rather than synchronizing with other swimmers, competitors synchronized with music.

2. **IN ANCIENT GREECE, WOMEN WERE NOT PERMITTED TO COMPETE IN THE OLYMPIC GAMES...BUT THEY HAD THEIR OWN VERSION OF THE EVENT, KNOWN AS THE "HERAEAN GAMES."**
Unfortunately, the event was much smaller, featuring only a few footraces for young women.

3. **UNFORTUNATELY, OLYMPIC ATHLETES (ALMOST ALWAYS WOMEN) HAVE OCCASIONALLY BEEN SUBJECTED TO "GENDER TESTING."**
In 1976, the UK's Princess Anne was competing in an equestrian event and was given special dispensation to avoid gender testing as it was viewed as inappropriate to test the Queen's daughter. Testing equestrian competitors seems particularly silly anyway—it's one of the rare events where men and women compete together!

4. **FOR SEVERAL DECADES BEGINNING IN 1912, THE OLYMPICS AWARDED MEDALS FOR ART IN EVENTS LIKE PAINTING, SCULPTING, AND ARCHITECTURE.**

5. ATHLETES AT THE OLYMPICS ARE COMMONLY PROVIDED WITH FREE CONDOMS, AS IT UNDERSTOOD THAT ATHLETES LIVING TOGETHER IN THE "OLYMPIC VILLAGE" WILL INEVITABLY HAVE SOME, AH, ROMANTIC ENTANGLEMENTS.

6. TRACK AND FIELD STAR WILMA RUDOLPH WON AN INCREDIBLE THREE GOLD MEDALS DURING THE 1960 OLYMPIC GAMES.

Her feat is made all the more impressive by the fact that she overcame childhood polio, which her doctor said would render her unable to ever walk—let alone run!

7. OLYMPIC GOLD MEDALS DO HAVE SOME GOLD IN THEM...BUT, HILARIOUSLY ENOUGH, THEY ARE MOSTLY MADE FROM SILVER.

8. ROMANIAN GYMNAST NADIA COMĂNECI WAS THE FIRST TO EVER SCORE A PERFECT 10 AT THE OLYMPICS.

This was commonly believed to be impossible—so much so that the scoreboard could not even display her score properly!

9. THE MOST DECORATED ATHLETE IN THE HISTORY OF THE PARALYMPIC GAMES IS SWIMMER TRISCHA ZORN.

Over her Paralympic career, she won an incredible 41 gold medals (and 55 medals overall).

· 10 ·

THE WINNER OF THE
1904 OLYMPIC MARATHON
WAS DISQUALIFIED WHEN
IT WAS DISCOVERED HE
HITCHED A RIDE IN A
CAR FOR 11 MILES.

• 11 •

FANNY BLANKERS-KOEN SET WORLD RECORDS IN THE LONG JUMP, HIGH JUMP, SPRINT, AND HURDLING EVENTS AT THE 1936 OLYMPIC GAMES.

She took 12 years off from Olympic competition, had two children, and returned to the games in 1948 to win four more gold medals!

12. IN 1976, SOVIET ATHLETE BORIS ONISHCHENKO WAS BANNED FROM FENCING FOR LIFE WHEN IT WAS DISCOVERED HE HAD WIRED HIS WEAPON TO REGISTER A TOUCH WITHOUT EVER ACTUALLY STRIKING HIS OPPONENT.

13. THE ORIGINAL OLYMPIC GAMES WERE BANNED IN 393 AD BY EMPEROR THEODOSIUS I, WHO SAW THEM AS A PAGAN FESTIVAL.
They weren't resumed until 1896!

14. DURING 1906 AND 1908, PISTOL DUELING WAS A SPORT AT THE OLYMPICS.
Fortunately, contestants competed using wax bullets and wore extensive protection.

15. IN AN ERA WHERE WORLD RECORDS ARE BROKEN ON A SEEMINGLY ANNUAL BASIS, IT IS PARTICULARLY IMPRESSIVE THAT THE HEPTATHLON WORLD RECORD SET BY LEGENDARY TRACK AND FIELD ATHLETE JACKIE JOYNER-KERSEE IN 1988 STILL STANDS TODAY.

16. DIMITRIOS LOUNDRAS REMAINS THE YOUNGEST COMPETITOR IN OLYMPIC HISTORY. IN 1896, HE COMPETED IN THE TEAM PARALLEL BARS EVENT AT THE AGE OF TEN.

17. **WOMEN DID NOT COMPETE IN THE FIRST MODERN OLYMPIC GAMES BECAUSE THE ORGANIZER, PIERRE DE COUBERTIN, BELIEVED THAT INCLUDING WOMEN WAS "IMPRACTICAL, UNINTERESTING, UNAESTHETIC, AND INCORRECT."**

Not exactly the most forward-thinking guy.

18. **OLYMPIC MEDALS ARE A MODERN INVENTION.**

In the ancient Olympic Games, the winner of each event was given an olive wreath, with no awards for second or third place.

19. **SOCCER WAS SUPPOSED TO BE AN EVENT AT THE 1896 OLYMPICS...BUT NONE OF THE TEAMS ACTUALLY SHOWED UP.**

Still, Denmark defeated Greece in an "unofficial" match to be crowned champions.

20. **THE ANCIENT OLYMPICS FEATURED A SPORT CALLED "PANKRATION," WHICH WAS AN "ANYTHING GOES" UNARMED COMBAT SPORT WHERE THE ONLY BANNED MOVES WERE BITING AND GOUGING.**

As you may expect, it was extremely brutal.

21. **AT THE OPENING CEREMONY OF THE 1992 OLYMPIC GAMES IN BARCELONA, PARALYMPIC ARCHER ANTONIO REBOLLO FIRED A FLAMING ARROW MORE THAN 230 FEET (70 METERS) WITH PERFECT AIM TO LIGHT THE OLYMPIC CAULDRON AT THE TOP OF THE STADIUM.**

• 22 •

IN 1936, TWO JAPANESE POLE VAULTERS TIED FOR SECOND PLACE. RATHER THAN COMPETING IN A TIEBREAKER, THE PAIR REFUSED TO CONTINUE SO THEY COULD SHARE THE PODIUM.

When they got back to Japan, they cut the silver and bronze medals in half and fused them together, so each could have a half silver, half bronze medal.

· 23 ·

CHRISTA ROTHENBURGER IS THE ONLY PERSON TO WIN A MEDAL IN THE SUMMER OLYMPICS AND THE WINTER OLYMPICS IN THE SAME YEAR.

She won gold in the women's 1,000 meter speed skating event in the 1988 Winter Olympic Games and later went on to earn the silver medal in track cycling during the summer.

· 24 ·

AMERICAN WOMEN
WERE NOT ALLOWED TO
COMPETE IN OLYMPIC
SWIMMING EVENTS UNTIL
1920, DUE TO AN ARCHAIC
RULE IN THE US THAT
STATED WOMEN HAD
TO WEAR FULL-LENGTH
SKIRTS DURING ANY
COMPETITION.

25. IN 1921, MONACO HOSTED THE FIRST JEUX OLYMPIQUES FÉMININS.

The event gave female athletes the opportunity to compete in the women's sports that had been excluded from the official Olympic Games.

26. "RACE WALKING" MADE ITS OLYMPIC DEBUT IN 1904.

The event is distinct from jogging or running in that one foot must always be in contact with the ground. Otherwise, a competitor is said to be "lifting."

27. THE TITLE OF "OLDEST OLYMPIAN" GOES TO OSCAR SWAHN OF SWEDEN, WHO WON HIS FIRST GOLD MEDAL AT AGE 60 IN THE RUNNING DEER SINGLE-SHOT EVENT IN 1908.

He returned after WWI to earn a silver medal at the ripe old age of 72.

28. THE POLARIZING MASCOT DUO OF THE 2012 LONDON OLYMPIC GAMES—WENLOCK AND MANDEVILLE—HAVE A FULL ORIGIN STORY DREAMED UP BY *WAR HORSE* AUTHOR MICHAEL MORPURGO:

They were said to be crafted from the last drops of steel used to create London's Olympic stadium by an elderly steel worker and brought to life by a rainbow.

29. HUNGARIAN FENCER PÁL SZEKERES IS REMARKABLE FOR BEING THE FIRST PERSON TO WIN MEDALS AT BOTH THE OLYMPIC GAMES AND AT THE PARALYMPIC GAMES, THE LATTER FOLLOWING A BUS ACCIDENT THAT RENDERED HIM WHEELCHAIR-BOUND.

30. THE 2020 OLYMPICS WERE A MILESTONE FOR TRANS-GENDER ATHLETES, AS NEW ZEALAND WEIGHTLIFTER LAUREL HUBBARD AND CANADIAN SOCCER PLAYER QUINN BECAME THE FIRST OPENLY TRANSGENDER ATHLETES TO PARTICIPATE IN THE OLYMPICS.
Nonbinary American skateboarder Alana Smith also joined them in helping to break down gender barriers.

31. THE ORIGIN OF THE PARALYMPIC GAMES CAN BE TRACED TO THE AFTERMATH OF WORLD WAR II AT A SPINAL INJURY REHABILITATION CENTER ESTABLISHED TO SERVE VETERANS.
German neurologist Sir Ludwig Guttman, who had fled Nazi Germany to England during the war, implemented recreational and then competitive sporting events at the Stoke Mandeville Hospital to help facilitate the recovery of injured servicemen and women.

32. IN 1936, THE FIRST-EVER OLYMPIC BASKETBALL FINAL WAS HELD ON AN OUTDOOR CLAY COURT THAT TURNED INTO A MUD PIT THANKS TO HEAVY RAIN.
The US defeated Canada by a paltry 19–8 score.

• 33 •

MARGARET MURDOCK TIED WITH US TEAM CAPTAIN LANNY BASSHAM IN THE 1976 SHOOTING COMPETITION, BUT TIEBREAKER RULES AWARDED HIM THE GOLD AND HER THE SILVER DESPITE BASSHAM'S REQUEST FOR A "SHOOT-OFF."

Frustrated by this, Bassham pulled Murdock up to share the gold-medal podium with him during the national anthem.

• 34 •

THE OLYMPIC TORCH
HAS BEEN TO SPACE.

Prior to the 2014 Summer Olympics,
the torch was passed between two
Russian cosmonauts while on a spacewalk.
Of course, it was not lit at the time.

· 35 ·

JOAN BENOIT SAMUELSON WON THE INAUGURAL WOMEN'S OLYMPIC MARATHON IN 1984.

What makes her feat even more impressive is that she had knee surgery just 17 days before the event!

36. THOUGH GIVEN THE OPTION TO DECLARE A HIGH JUMP WINNER VIA A JUMP-OFF AT THE 2020 TOKYO GAMES, MUTAZ ESSA BARSHIM OF QATAR AND GIANMARCO TAMBERI OF ITALY DECIDED INSTEAD TO SHARE THEIR GOLD MEDAL WHEN THE COMPETITION RESULTED IN A TIE.

The moment proved an inspiring display of sportsmanship.

37. THERE ARE ONLY TWO SPORTS THAT EXIST EXCLUSIVELY IN THE PARALYMPICS, WITHOUT AN OLYMPIC COUNTERPART: GOALBALL AND BOCCIA.

Goalball is a team sport created in the wake of WWII to help blind veterans stay active and involves rolling a ball containing bells over the opponent's goal line. Boccia is designed for athletes with motor skill impairments and involves throwing or rolling colored balls as close to a target as possible.

38. BILLY MILLS'S VICTORY IN THE 1964 OLYMPIC 10,000-METER RUN IS CONSIDERED ONE OF THE GREATEST UPSETS OF ALL TIME.

Mills was born on a reservation for the Oglala Lakota people and never owned a pair of new shoes until just before the Olympics began.

39. **THE 100TH GOLD MEDAL IN AUSTRALIAN OLYMPIC HISTORY HAD A SPECIAL SIGNIFICANCE: IT WAS WON BY CATHY FREEMAN DURING THE 2000 OLYMPICS (WHICH WERE HOSTED BY AUSTRALIA), AND IT MADE HER THE FIRST ABORIGINAL AUSTRALIAN TO WIN AN INDIVIDUAL GOLD.**

Just eight years before, Freeman had become the first Aboriginal Australian to compete in the Olympics at all!

40. **THE FIRST OLYMPIC LOSS EVER SUFFERED BY THE US MEN'S BASKETBALL TEAM OCCURRED UNDER HIGHLY SUSPICIOUS CIRCUMSTANCES:**

Officials allowed the final three seconds of the 1972 final to be replayed three times, until the Soviet team prevailed on a last-second basket. To this day, the US team has refused to accept its silver medal out of protest.

41. **TRUE OR FALSE: NO OLYMPICS HOST NATION HAS EVER FAILED TO WIN A GOLD MEDAL DURING COMPETITION.**

FALSE. Canada did not win a single gold medal at the 1976 Summer Olympics. It is the only time in Summer Olympics history that the host nation has failed to win a gold medal.

· 42 ·

TRUE OR FALSE: ABEBE BIKILA, THE WINNER OF THE MEN'S MARATHON AT THE 1960 SUMMER OLYMPICS, SET A WORLD RECORD DESPITE RUNNING THE ENTIRE RACE BAREFOOT.

TRUE. Even more impressively, the Ethiopian runner was the first sub-Saharan African to win a gold medal at the Olympics.

43. TRUE OR FALSE: FIGURE SKATING WAS ORIGINALLY A SUMMER OLYMPICS SPORT, NOT A WINTER OLYMPICS SPORT.

TRUE. Figure skating predates the Winter Olympics, but was moved to the winter games upon their inception.

44. TRUE OR FALSE: EQUATOGUINEAN SWIMMER ERIC MOUSSAMBANI SET THE RECORD FOR THE FASTEST TIME IN THE 100M FREESTYLE SWIMMING EVENT DESPITE NEVER HAVING SEEN AN OLYMPIC-SIZED POOL PRIOR TO THE GAMES.

FALSE. The bit about the pool is true, but Moussambani's time is actually the slowest winning time in history. Fortunately for him, it didn't matter: both of his competitors were disqualified, and he swam his heat alone! (Sadly, he did not advance to the next round.)

45. TRUE OR FALSE: A SOVIET WATER POLO PLAYER ONCE PUNCHED AN OPPONENT IN THE FACE IN THE MIDDLE OF A MATCH.

TRUE. Valentin Prokopov punched his Hungarian opponent Ervin Zádor, leaving blood streaming down his face. The event became known as the "Blood in the Water" match. The incident was considered emblematic of Cold War tensions at the time.

46. TRUE OR FALSE: DESPITE RUMORS THAT ANCIENT OLYMPIC ATHLETES COMPETED IN THE NUDE, MOST WORE TOGAS OR OTHER MODEST COVERINGS.

FALSE. Nope, they really did compete in the nude!

47. TRUE OR FALSE: IN 1998, AN OLYMPIC JUDGE SECRETLY RECORDED A FELLOW JUDGE ATTEMPTING TO DICTATE THE RESULTS OF THE GYMNASTICS COMPETITION BEFORE IT TOOK PLACE.

FALSE. This did happen, but the event wasn't gymnastics—it was ice dancing. It very nearly led to the sport being entirely removed from Olympic competition.

48. TRUE OR FALSE: IN 2000, CHINESE GYMNAST DONG FANGXIAO WAS DISQUALIFIED AFTER IT WAS REVEALED SHE LIED ABOUT HER AGE, CLAIMING TO BE YOUNGER THAN SHE ACTUALLY WAS.

FALSE. In fact, she claimed to be older than she was: Dong was just 14 at the time, below the acceptable age for Olympic competition. She would not be the last Chinese gymnast caught competing underage.

49. TRUE OR FALSE: THE FIRST TWO WOMEN'S BASKETBALL EVENTS WERE NOT WON BY THE US, BUT BY THE SOVIET UNION.

TRUE. While the US is generally considered the dominant force in basketball, that hasn't always been the case in women's basketball. When women's basketball was added to Olympic competition, the Soviet Union women's team won the first two gold medals in 1976 and 1980. In 1992, the "Unified" team (which included Russia) won gold once more.

· 50 ·

TRUE OR FALSE: A ONE-LEGGED GYMNAST ONCE CLAIMED VICTORY IN MULTIPLE OLYMPIC EVENTS.

TRUE. American gymnast George Eyser won six medals in 1906, despite the fact that he had a wooden leg!

[Miscellaneous]

Sports like football, soccer, and basketball may be among the world's most popular, but there are plenty of other sports that deserve some attention. In fact, sports like golf, boxing, and tennis could probably fill entire sections of their own. Others, like skiing, chess, and toe wrestling (yes, you're reading that right), could not. This section is for the miscellaneous sports facts that don't fit into any of the "major" sports but are sure to delight you nonetheless.

1. **THE FASTEST KNOCKOUT IN THE HISTORY OF MMA FIGHTING TOOK JUST TWO SECONDS.**
Good luck breaking that record!

2. **PRESIDENT ABRAHAM LINCOLN IS IN THE WRESTLING HALL OF FAME. IN HIS CAREER AS A WRESTLER, HE HAS ONLY ONE RECORDED DEFEAT IN 300 MATCHES!**

3. **DURING A WOMEN'S TENNIS MATCH IN 1984, VICKI NELSON-DUNBAR AND JEAN HEPNER ENGAGED IN A 643-SHOT RALLY THAT TOOK 29 MINUTES TO COMPLETE.**
It was the longest competitive rally in the history of the sport.

4. **IN NORTH AMERICAN SPORTS, JUST FIVE TEAMS HAVE EVER WON A PLAYOFF SERIES AFTER TRAILING BY THREE GAMES (THE 1942 TORONTO MAPLE LEAFS, THE 1975 NEW YORK ISLANDERS, THE 2004 BOSTON RED SOX, THE 2010 PHILADELPHIA FLYERS, AND THE 2014 LOS ANGELES KINGS).**
The feat has never been achieved in the NBA.

5. **DURING A 2016 RYDER CUP PRACTICE ROUND, A GROUP OF EUROPEAN GOLFERS GOT TIRED OF BEING HECKLED BY AN AMERICAN FAN OVER THEIR POOR PUTTING.**
They bet the fan $100 that he couldn't sink the same putt... but, unfortunately for them, the fan was up to the challenge, sinking the shot and walking away with his head held high.

6. DURING THE 1935 BIG TEN CHAMPIONSHIPS, JESSE OWENS SET AN INCREDIBLE FIVE WORLD RECORDS IN JUST 45 MINUTES.

7. IN 1949, PROFESSIONAL BOXER GUS WALDORF FOUGHT A BEAR WEARING BOXING GLOVES (YES—THE BEAR WAS WEARING SPECIAL BEAR-SIZED BOXING GLOVES).
The bear won by K.O.

8. IN 1923, A JOCKEY NAMED FRANK HAYNES WON A HORSE RACE DESPITE THE FACT THAT HAYNES HAD DIED FROM A HEART ATTACK DURING THE RACE.

9. TENNIS PLAYERS WHO REACH THE QUARTERFINALS AT WIMBLEDON ARE WELCOMED INTO THE "LAST 8 CLUB." THE CLUB COMES WITH A NUMBER OF PERKS, INCLUDING FREE WIMBLEDON TICKETS FOR LIFE AND FREE TEA THROUGHOUT THE EVENT.

10. AMERICAN DARA TORRES BECAME THE OLDEST SWIMMER TO WIN AN OLYMPIC GOLD MEDAL WHEN SHE COMPETED IN THE 2000 OLYMPICS AT THE AGE OF 33.
Not satisfied, she returned for the 2008 Olympics, where she won three more medals at age 41!

• 11 •

THE ROMAN COLOSSEUM
WASN'T JUST USED
FOR GLADIATOR FIGHTS
AND CHARIOT RACES: IT
WAS ONCE FILLED WITH
WATER AND USED TO
CONDUCT A GIANT MOCK
NAVAL BATTLE.

· 12 ·

AT THE AGE OF 27, GYMNAST SIMONE BILES WON HER RECORD NINTH NATIONAL ALL-AROUND TITLE AT THE US GYMNASTICS CHAMPIONSHIPS.

Two months later, she won gold in the Olympic all-around finals (for the second time!). She is the most decorated gymnast in history and many consider her to be the greatest gymnast of all time.

13. SIMONE BILES IS SO DOMINANT IN HER SPORT THAT THERE ARE FIVE ELEMENTS IN THE WOMEN'S ARTISTIC GYMNASTIC CODE OF POINTS NAMED AFTER HER—SO FAR!

14. IN 2012, THE EUROPEAN CHESS UNION ADOPTED AN INTERESTING RULE FOR WOMEN'S CHESS TOURNAMENTS: THEY SPECIFICALLY STIPULATED HOW MANY BUTTONS COULD BE OPEN ON A CONTESTANT'S SHIRT.

Effectively, the ECU banned cleavage.

15. IN THE LATE 1800S, COMPETITIVE WALKING—DUBBED "PEDESTRIANISM"—BECAME A POPULAR NATIONAL SPORTING EVENT, WITH SOME WALKING MATCHES LASTING FOR SIX STRAIGHT DAYS AND REQUIRING COMPETITORS TO WALK LAPS AROUND AN INDOOR TRACK, DAY AND NIGHT, UNTIL THEY REACHED A CUMULATIVE DISTANCE OF UP TO 450 MILES.

16. RUSSIA'S NATALIA MOLCHANOVA IS WIDELY CONSIDERED TO BE THE GREATEST FREE DIVER IN HISTORY.

At the time of her death, she held an amazing 41 free diving world records, and was the first woman in history to reach a depth of 100 meters without the use of weights.

17. THE WORLD'S LONGEST CERTIFIED FOOT RACE, CALLED THE SRI CHINMOY SELF-TRANSCENDENCE 3,100 MILE RACE, TAKES PLACE IN QUEENS, NY. Named for the Indian spiritual leader who founded it, the event requires runners to circle a single block from 6 a.m. to midnight for up to 52 straight days until they reach the 3,100-mile distance.

18. BALTIMORE-NATIVE EXTREME ATHLETE STEVE MCKINNEY—DUBBED THE "HIGH PRIEST OF SPEED SKIING"—WAS BOTH THE FIRST SPEED SKIER TO BREAK THE 200 KPH BARRIER, AND THE FIRST PERSON TO HANG GLIDE OFF MOUNT EVEREST.

19. WHEELCHAIR TENNIS STAR ESTHER VERGEER WAS UNDEFEATED IN SINGLES MATCHES FOR MORE THAN TEN YEARS, ENDING HER CAREER WITH AN ASTONISHING STREAK OF 470 CONSECUTIVE WINS.

20. AMERICAN ALPINE SKIER MIKAELA SHIFFRIN IS ONE OF THE MOST ACCOMPLISHED SKIERS IN HISTORY. By the age of 29, she had already won more Alpine Ski World Cup events than any competitor in history, men or women— and she probably isn't finished.

21. IN 1926, GERTRUDE EDERLE WAS JUST 19 YEARS OLD WHEN SHE BECAME THE FIRST WOMAN TO SWIM ACROSS THE ENGLISH CHANNEL, A 21-MILE JOURNEY.

· 22 ·

MILDRED "BABE" DIDRIKSON ZAHARIAS WAS A CELEBRATED TRACK AND FIELD ATHLETE WHO WON TWO GOLD MEDALS AND A SILVER MEDAL AT THE 1932 OLYMPICS.

She later became a professional golfer and proceeded to win ten LPGA major championships. Zaharias was also known as an excellent baseball and basketball player.

· 23 ·

OIL WRESTLING IS A WILDLY POPULAR SPORT IN TURKEY, AND IT'S EXACTLY WHAT IT SOUNDS LIKE.

In fact, there's a multiday oil wrestling festival held annually in Edirne that originated in the 1300s and still continues to this day. In this event steeped in ritual, up to 2,000 competitors don leather shorts, slather themselves in olive oil, and vie for the title of Chief Wrestler.

24. IT'S A KNOWN FACT THAT WAXING YOUR SKIS CAN HELP BOOST YOUR SPEED, AND MANY CREATIVE WAX PREPARATIONS HAVE BEEN DOCUMENTED THROUGHOUT HISTORY, INCLUDING THE APPLICATION OF HUMAN SEMEN TO THE UNDERSIDE OF SKIS IN THE 19TH CENTURY.

25. THE MARATHON MONKS OF MOUNT HIEI APPROACH WALKING AND RUNNING AS A FORM OF MEDITATION THROUGH MOVEMENT IN A QUEST TO REACH ENLIGHTENMENT, WORKING TOWARD THE GOAL OF COMPLETING 1,000 DAYS OF LONG-DISTANCE RUNNING OVER A STRICTLY REGIMENTED SEVEN-YEAR PERIOD.
Only 46 monks have ever completed this 1,000-day challenge.

26. IN A RECENT STUDY THAT EXAMINED LONG-DISTANCE OPEN-WATER SWIMMING TIMES, WOMEN WERE FOUND TO SWIM THE ENGLISH CHANNEL ABOUT 33 MINUTES FASTER THAN MEN ON AVERAGE.

27. SORRY, LEFTIES—THE UNITED STATES POLO ASSOCIATION MAINTAINS A RULING THAT ONLY RIGHT-HANDED PLAYING IS ALLOWED.

28. THE LONGEST RECORDED CRICKET MATCH TOOK PLACE IN 1939 BETWEEN ENGLAND AND SOUTH AFRICA AND SPANNED MORE THAN 43 HOURS OF PLAYTIME.

29. SQUASH LEGEND HEATHER MCKAY RETIRED IN 1981 AFTER ALMOST 20 YEARS OF UNDEFEATED PLAY. She won an incredible 16 consecutive British Open titles in the 60s and 70s and is widely considered to be the greatest female player in the history of the game.

30. TRAILBLAZING RACECAR DRIVER JANET GUTHRIE OWNS THREE MAJOR RECORDS IN PROFESSIONAL DRIVING: SHE'S THE FIRST WOMAN EVER TO COMPETE IN THE INDY 500 AND THE DAYTONA 500, AND THE FIRST FEMALE DRIVER TO COMPETE IN A NASCAR SUPERSPEEDWAY RACE.

31. THE CURRENT WORLD RECORD HOLDER FOR SPEEDIEST SOLO SAIL AROUND THE GLOBE IS FRENCH SAILOR FRANÇOIS GABART, WHO COMPLETED THE SOLO JOURNEY IN JUST UNDER 43 DAYS USING NATURAL FORCES ONLY. That's right—no engines.

32. THE OLDEST CONTINUOUSLY HELD SPORTING EVENT IN THE UNITED STATES IS THE KENTUCKY DERBY, WHICH HASN'T SKIPPED A BEAT SINCE IT LAUNCHED IN 1875.

33. EVER SINCE 1905, THE SAME WHISTLE HAS BEEN USED TO START EVERY RUGBY WORLD CUP. That thing has to be pretty gross by now.

• 34 •

IN 2010, SPANISH MOUNTAINEER EDURNE PASABAN BECAME THE FIRST WOMAN TO SCALE ALL 8,000-FOOT MOUNTAINS IN THE WORLD.

The first 8,000 footer she tackled? Mount Everest—at the age of 28!

THE ANNUAL COOPER'S
HILL CHEESE-ROLLING
AND WAKE CHALLENGES
COMPETITORS TO RACE
DOWN A 200-YARD HILL
IN PURSUIT OF A 7- TO
8-POUND WHEEL OF
DOUBLE GLOUCESTER
CHEESE THAT, PERHAPS
UNFAIRLY, IS GIVEN A ONE-
SECOND HEAD START.

36. THE ICONIC BORG-WARNER TROPHY THAT IS PRESENTED TO THE WINNER OF THE INDY 500 WEIGHS IN AT OVER 110 POUNDS AND FEATURES A BAS-RELIEF PORTRAIT OF EVERY CHAMPION TO DATE.

The new base that was added to accommodate these winning likenesses will be filled to capacity in 2034.

37. FINLAND HAS HOSTED AN ANNUAL WIFE-CARRYING COMPETITION SINCE THE 1990S, IN WHICH ENTRANTS ENDEAVOR TO COMPLETE AN OBSTACLE COURSE WITH THEIR PARTNER ON THEIR BACK IN THE SHORTEST AMOUNT OF TIME.

38. DURING THE 1988 OLYMPIC TRIALS AND OLYMPICS, RUNNER FLORENCE GRIFFITH JOYNER SET WORLD RECORDS IN THE 100-METER SPRINT AND 200-METER SPRINT—BOTH OF WHICH STILL STAND MORE THAN THREE DECADES LATER.

39. IS IT TECHNICALLY A SPORT IF ONLY THREE PEOPLE ARE ENGAGED IN IT?

A trio of UK-based cellists created an activity called "Extreme Cello" in which they perform while scaling mountains, walking great distances, or even while running a marathon.

40. EVERY KID HAS ENGAGED IN THUMB WRESTLING, BUT DID YOU KNOW THERE IS A FOOT-BASED ALTERNATIVE KNOWN AS TOE WRESTLING?

It has a world championship and everything!

41. LEGENDARY RUSSIAN POLE VAULTER YELENA ISINBAEVA BECAME THE FIRST WOMAN TO CLEAR A FIVE-METER BAR IN 2005.

Amid her quest, she broke her own world record not once, not twice, but 28 times!

42. THE FIRST-PERSON ACTION FILM *HARDCORE HENRY* WAS SHOT WITH CUSTOM GOPRO RIGS WORN BY THE PERFORMERS.

The filmmaker hired a parkour expert to wear the rig like a mask to perform the most intense scenes that called for scaling a wall or leaping from a great height.

43. NATHAN'S HOT DOG-EATING CONTEST HAS BEEN TAK-ING PLACE ANNUALLY ON CONEY ISLAND SINCE 1972 AND ATTRACTS NEARLY 40,000 SPECTATORS EACH YEAR TO WATCH COMPETITORS GOBBLE UP AS MANY HOT DOGS AS THEY CAN IN TEN SHORT MINUTES.

Reigning champ Joey Chestnut set a new record in 2021 by eating 76 hot dogs before time was up.

44. THERE'S A REASON FORMULA ONE CARS ARE PRACTICALLY THE STUFF OF LEGEND IN THE AUTOMOTIVE WORLD: THE AVERAGE F1 CAR IS ESTIMATED TO ACCELERATE FROM 0 TO 60 MILES PER HOUR IN AS LITTLE AS 2.5 SECONDS— AND SOMETIMES EVEN FASTER.

· 45 ·

A ONE-ARMED TENNIS PLAYER NAMED HANS REDL ONCE REACHED THE FOURTH ROUND OF WIMBLEDON.

He was given special permission to touch the ball with his racket prior to serving in order to throw the ball into the air.

· 46 ·

KATHRINE SWITZER BECAME THE FIRST WOMAN TO OFFICIALLY COMPETE IN THE BOSTON MARATHON WHEN SHE REGISTERED USING HER INITIALS, K. V., TO DISGUISE HER GENDER.

Upon realizing that a woman had registered, race organizer Jock Semple became so irate that he attempted to rip her numbers off after just four miles. With the help of fellow runners, Switzer was able to evade Semple and become the first woman to finish the race. Amazingly, Switzer and Semple would later become friends.

47. THE OLDEST DRIVER TO COMPETE IN THE WORLD RALLY CHAMPIONSHIP, THE PREMIER RALLYING COMPETITION, WAS SOBIESŁAW ZASADA, A 91-YEAR-OLD DRIVER FROM POLAND. SADLY, COLLISIONS ON THE COURSE PREVENTED HIM FROM FINISHING THE RACE.

48. EVER WANTED TO EXPERIENCE A DAY IN THE LIFE OF A FLORIDA MAN (LIKE THE ONES YOU SEE IN THE HEADLINES)?

February 2024 saw the debut of the Florida Man Games in St. Augustine, featuring competitive events like "Beer Belly Florida Sumo" and the "Evading Arrest Obstacle Course."

49. IN ADDITION TO HAVING AN ABSOLUTELY INCREDIBLE NAME, LIBBY RIDDLES BECAME THE FIRST WOMAN TO WIN THE FAMED IDITAROD TRAIL SLED DOG RACE WHEN SHE AND HER TEAM OF DOGS LEFT THEIR COMPETITORS IN THE DUST (POWDER?) IN 1985.

50. SWIMMER DIANA NYAD BOASTS SOME OF THE MOST IMPRESSIVE ACCOMPLISHMENTS IN HISTORY.

She once made the 102-mile swim from the Bahamas to Florida, and became just the third person to swim the 110-mile journey from Havana, Cuba to Key West, Florida. The kicker? She did it at the age of 64.

51. TONGAN RUGBY PLAYER EPI TAIONE LEGALLY CHANGED HIS NAME TO "PADDY POWER" FOR THE 2007 RUGBY WORLD CUP AFTER AGREEING TO A SPONSORSHIP DEAL WITH THE WELL-KNOWN GAMBLING COMPANY.

52. NASCAR LEGEND RICHARD PETTY'S FIRST-EVER WIN WAS TAKEN AWAY WHEN ANOTHER DRIVER PROTESTED THAT THERE HAD BEEN A SCORING ERROR. THAT DRIVER? RICHARD'S DAD, LEE PETTY.

53. NINE-PIN BOWLING WAS ONCE BANNED THROUGHOUT THE UNITED STATES.

As a result, ten-pin bowling emerged as a way to technically circumvent the law.

54. LEGENDARY BOXER SUGAR RAY ROBINSON ALMOST BACKED OUT OF A FIGHT BECAUSE HE HAD A DREAM THAT HE KILLED HIS OPPONENT, JIMMY DOYLE, IN THE RING.

A priest and a minister ultimately convinced Robinson to fight... but Robinson's dream became a reality and Doyle was killed.

55. THE FASTEST RECORDED OBJECT IN SPORTS HISTORY IS NONE OTHER THAN THE SHUTTLECOCK: Tan Boon Hoeng of Malaysia smacked a badminton birdie and recorded a speed of 306 miles per hour in a controlled environment, a record that hasn't yet been beaten.

56. DURING A 2017 NASCAR RACE, AN AMBULANCE INADVERTENTLY CAUSED AN ACCIDENT WHEN IT WOUND UP ON PIT ROW AT AN INOPPORTUNE TIME.

57. LONGTIME FORMULA ONE RACERS GERHARD BERGER AND AYRTON SENNA HAD A LEGENDARY PRANK WAR.

Berger once filled Senna's hotel room with frogs the night before a race.

58. DURING HIS FIRST RACE AFTER SWITCHING TEAMS FROM MCLAREN TO MERCEDES, LEGENDARY DRIVER LEWIS HAMILTON ACCIDENTALLY PULLED INTO THE MCLAREN PIT LANE RATHER THAN HIS OWN.

59. FORMER FORMULA ONE RACER ROBERT DOORNBOS TRADED IN ONE TYPE OF HIGH-PERFORMANCE MACHINE FOR ANOTHER: NOW RETIRED FROM RACING, DOORNBOS COFOUNDED AN ADULT TOY COMPANY.

60. CHEATING HAS BEEN A PART OF THE TOUR DE FRANCE FROM THE VERY BEGINNING: DURING THE FIRST COMPETITION IN 1903, MULTIPLE RIDERS WERE SANCTIONED FOR ILLEGAL BEHAVIOR—INCLUDING THE EVENTUAL WINNER.

The next year, in 1904, multiple riders were disqualified after they were found hopping a train!

61. TRUE OR FALSE: IT IS ILLEGAL TO USE YOUR FEET TO STRIKE THE BALL IN VOLLEYBALL.

FALSE. While it was illegal for much of the sport's history, as of 1999, volleyball players are permitted to use their feet if they so choose.

62. TRUE OR FALSE: CRICKET USED TO BE POPULAR IN THE UNITED STATES, AND GEORGE WASHINGTON IS EVEN BELIEVED TO HAVE PLAYED IT.

TRUE. While cricket never fully took off in the US, it was more popular than it is today. Washington reportedly played a game called "wickets" with his troops, believed to have been based on cricket.

63. TRUE OR FALSE: THE FIRST INTERNATIONAL SPORTING MATCH IN THE WORLD WAS AN 1831 SOCCER MATCH BETWEEN THE US AND MEXICO.

FALSE. Actually, it was an 1844 cricket match between the US and Canada!

64. TRUE OR FALSE: NO NASCAR DRIVER HAS EVER WON A RACE WHILE LAPPING THE ENTIRE FIELD.

FALSE. It is rare, though. It last happened in 1994, when Geoff Bodine lapped the field during the 1994 Tyson Holly Farms 400.

65. TRUE OR FALSE: WHEN RACER PEDRO RODRÍGUEZ WON THE 1967 SOUTH AFRICAN GRAND PRIX, THE RACE ORGANIZERS DID NOT HAVE A COPY OF THE MEXICAN NATIONAL ANTHEM, SO THEY PLAYED THE "MEXICAN HAT DANCE" INSTEAD.

TRUE. This is, regrettably, true. Rodríguez reportedly never traveled without a Mexican flag and copy of the anthem after that.

· 66 ·

TRUE OR FALSE: A FEMALE BOXER ONCE KNOCKED OUT A MALE FIGHTER AT A MADISON SQUARE GARDEN EVENT.

TRUE. Famed boxer Jackie Tonawanda (known to many as "the female Muhammad Ali") was so determined to fight men that she sued for the right to do it. In 1975, she got her wish and knocked out kickboxer Larry Rodania after just two rounds in front of a Madison Square Garden crowd.

67. **TRUE OR FALSE: A FORMULA ONE DRIVER WAS ONCE DISQUALIFIED FROM A RACE FOR DRIVING TOO SLOWLY.**

TRUE. In 1969, driver Al Pease was disqualified for driving at "excessively low speeds," which caused a danger to himself and other racers.

68. **TRUE OR FALSE: THE FAMOUSLY LEFT-HANDED RAFAEL NADAL IS ACTUALLY RIGHT-HANDED BUT LEARNED TO PLAY TENNIS AS A LEFTY FOLLOWING A CHILDHOOD INJURY.**

FALSE. While it's true that Nadal is naturally right-handed, he gravitated toward left-handed play. He also plays soccer with a dominant left foot.

69. **TRUE OR FALSE: SEBASTIAN VETTEL SET A FORMULA ONE RECORD WHEN HE WAS PENALIZED JUST SIX MINUTES INTO HIS DEBUT RACE.**

FALSE. It's true that he set the record, but it didn't take him six minutes: he was penalized for speeding just nine seconds into his first race!

70. **TRUE OR FALSE: LEFT-HANDED STICKS ARE BANNED IN FIELD HOCKEY.**

TRUE. The sticks are deemed a safety hazard due to the way the game is played. In sanctioned competitions and tournaments, only right-handed sticks can be used.

71. TRUE OR FALSE: BOXER NEL TARLETON BECAME THE BRITISH FEATHERWEIGHT CHAMPION THREE SEPARATE TIMES DESPITE BEING BORN WITH AN EXTRA LUNG.

FALSE. Actually, Tarleton had just one lung from a very young age.

72. TRUE OR FALSE: LACROSSE IS CONSIDERED THE OLDEST SPORT IN NORTH AMERICA.

TRUE. Lacrosse was originally invented and played by a number of Native American tribes. It is believed to date back as early as the 1100s.

73. TRUE OR FALSE: TENNIS'S STRANGE SCORING SYSTEM WAS THE WORK OF A FAMOUSLY MAD KING OF ENGLAND AT THE TIME OF ITS INVENTION.

FALSE. Actually, no one is quite sure why tennis's "15, 30, 40" scoring system emerged. The most common theory holds that scores were originally kept using clock faces.

74. TRUE OR FALSE: TENNIS BALLS WERE ORIGINALLY WHITE OR BLACK, AND YELLOW BALLS ONLY ENTERED PLAY AFTER THE INVENTION OF COLOR TELEVISION.

TRUE. In fact, Sir David Attenborough, who was a controller for the BBC at the time, was among those who pushed for the change.

• 75 •

TRUE OR FALSE: EARLY IN THE TOUR DE FRANCE'S HISTORY, IT WAS COMMON FOR RIDERS TO "RAID" BARS AND CAFES ALONG THE ROUTE, STEALING ALCOHOL AND OTHER BEVERAGES.

TRUE. Funny as this is, it was ultimately self-defeating: since alcohol dehydrates the body, they were only hurting themselves.

Acknowledgments

A trivia book demands a significant amount of research, and I am profoundly grateful to the many, many sources of weird and wonderful sports and athletics-related facts that helped me through this journey. I use multiple sources to verify every fact, and the following were among the most helpful. A warm and hearty thank you to:

- ESPN
- Sports Reference
- SB Nation (especially Jon Bois)
- The Athletic
- Sports Illustrated
- USA Today
- Complex
- Bleacher Report
- NPR
- Goal
- The Guardian
- The Guinness Book of World Records
- Every sports "Hall of Fame" under the sun
- The NFL, MLB, NBA, NHL, NCAA, IOC, and FIFA (among other leagues and governing bodies)
- Wikipedia (which was often an excellent starting point)
- Snopes (to bust some of the peskier myths)
- …and countless others

But finally, a thank you to the many denizens of social media, including X (formerly known as Twitter) and Reddit. Your facts weren't always correct, but even the wrong ones sent me down fun and fruitful rabbit holes.

ABOUT
SHANE CARLEY

Shane Carley lives deep in the woods of Western Massachusetts, hammering away on his keyboard between trips to walk the dog and feed the chickens. When he isn't researching obscure trivia to include in his next book, he is probably experimenting with new cocktail recipes for his highly popular Home Bartender book series. In his other life, Shane spearheads content development for an award-winning public relations firm, where he helps ensure his clients' words do not, in fact, sound like *bull$#*t*.

ABOUT CIDER MILL PRESS BOOK PUBLISHERS

Good ideas ripen with time.
From seed to harvest, Cider Mill Press
brings fine reading, information, and
entertainment together between the covers
of its creatively crafted books. Our Cider
Mill bears fruit twice a year, publishing a
new crop of titles each spring and fall.

"Where Good Books Are Ready for Press"
501 Nelson Place
Nashville, Tennessee 37214
cidermillpress.com